The Power of Switchwords

Franziska Krattinger

THE POWER OF SWITCHWORDS

67 Words to Reprogram Your Life

EARTHDANCER

AN INNER TRADITIONS IMPRINT

Disclaimer

The information in this book is given in good faith and is not intended to diagnose any physical or mental condition or serve as a substitute for informed medical advice or care. Please contact your health professional for medical advice and treatment. Neither author nor publisher can be held liable by any person for any loss or damage whatsoever that may arise from the use of this book or any of the information therein.

First edition 2022
The Power of Switchwords
67 Words to Reprogram Your Life
Franziska Krattinger

This English edition © 2022 Earthdancer GmbH
English translation © 2022 JMS books LLP
Editing by JMS books LLP (www.jmseditorial.com)

Originally published in German as: *Ein Wort genügt!... sich einfach umprogrammieren*
World © 2006 Verlag "Die Silberschnur" GmbH, Güllesheim, Germany

Cover Illustration: Kanaa/vectorstock.com
Cover design: Aaron Davis
Typesetting and layout: Chris Bell
Typeset in Archer
Printed and bound in China by Reliance Printing Co., Ltd.

ISBN 978-1-64411-677-7 (print)
ISBN 978-1-64411-678-4 (ebook)

Cataloging-in-Publication Data for this title is available from the Library of Congress.

Published by Earthdancer, an imprint of Inner Traditions
www.earthdancerbooks.com, www.innertraditions.com

CONTENTS

INTRODUCTION

A single word can speak volumes. A brief message can have a long and deep resonance. The essence of what we say is often lost or diluted in long sentences and more complicated explanations.

A single word uttered in the right place at the right time will have a lasting effect. It therefore makes sense to pay close attention to the meaning and effect of each word and to choose them accordingly. Each word carries its own reverberations. Words are the key to specific energies. They elicit actions and reactions, so it is important to pay attention to those that you choose to use.

The practical guide to switchwords in the second part of this book explains how to use switchwords to their best effect.

THE BASICS

Your Switchword Toolkit

*Remember that you can never change
another person (you can only change yourself),
but you can always change a situation!*

"I am the way"

Countless people labor under the mistaken belief that someone else is responsible for the situations in which they find themselves. If they persist in this attitude, however, they will never experience the fundamental life change they are hoping for, instead remaining convinced that they are dependent upon the specific actions of others and that there is little that can be done about it. They wait in vain for those around them to change so that change may occur in their own lives. This mindset stops the individual from taking action. Personal attitudes are the deciding factor and also the yardstick by which an outcome can be measured.

Once we focus our attention on ourselves and on finding a solution for our situation, a path of action becomes clear. What other people think is not the determining factor, but rather what we think and want to do. Mental powerlessness comes to define our daily existence. Others continue to distract us and we realize we are not in control or in a position to find the necessary solutions to issues, leaving us open to challenging emotions such as desperation, rage, irritability, dissatisfaction, frustration, anger, helplessness, and negativity.

Are there times when you feel tired and at the end of your tether, completely out of kilter with things and unable to get back on an even keel? Sometimes it seems as though we are surrounded by crazy, unstable people because we too have been knocked off-center; we are no longer calm and balanced, no longer in a place where we can see everything clearly for what it is and are unable to grasp the solutions that are available. We have been led to believe that we are dependent on the particular actions of others and are therefore unable to do or change much ourselves. This idea, along with an unchallenging acceptance of situations, is a deep-seated attitude for many people, who become annoyed at the behavior of others while at the same time forgetting their own power and agency. They have brought about their own circumstances, which only they can change, but they frequently hinder their own attempts to do so by believing external forces are to blame. Their quality of life is determined by the behavior of their fellow humans, and they think they must obey the dictates of external influences. Other people, situations, and circumstances may appear to be the cause of the difficulties and challenges they face, but in fact these are no more than a reflection of their own internalized way of looking at the world and their deep-rooted perspective on reality. "Change yourself and life will change!"

The deciding factor is therefore our own attitude. It underpins the real-world outcome and is something to which we should pay particular attention and monitor closely.

If we do not focus on ourselves and our attitudes, our mistakes will simply persist, along with the problems that arise from them. It is easy to become stuck in a rut and allow the behavior of others to annoy us, becoming short-tempered and angry for no real reason. Feeling critical of others provokes negative emotions within us. Being fixated on this "other" way of life stops us from carrying on with our own approach to life. The world around us mirrors our behavior. If we ask ourselves what it is within us that causes such things to happen, we can begin to unlock our inner potential for change. We are our own solution. Situations and circumstances may appear to have ground to a halt or to be "stuck," but it is our own attitude that is causing the blockage. So take responsibility for everything that happens in life. The most important thing is to overcome negative emotions and feelings, to simply get rid of them, banish them from our consciousness. If we change our value system, we can manifest our true values. This is the beginning of genuine and real change. We must free ourselves of all that stands in the way of being happy and blessed. Instead of believing we can change nothing, let's start changing the things that can indeed be changed right now.

Focus on your options. Take stock of whatever you are rejecting or declining, since this will continue to get in your way. Every refusal is a distraction. Every doubt robs you of mental power. Be aware of your own agency; your truth lies within. This is the path and the key to true fulfillment: focus on your own behavior and you will recognize where change will be to your benefit. Self-awareness is the path to true liberation. Your abilities and strengths will grow with time, and you will find it increasingly easy to achieve what you want in the real world.

Never forget that you are in a position to make possible the impossible. Keep this at the forefront of your mind and it will work its magic.

We all determine our own paths through the thoughts that engage the mind and provoke reactions. Thoughts are forces of energetic momentum that manifest themselves in real-life situations and lived experiences. Our tools are love and the power of our thoughts. This is the ideal combination, embodying the greatest and highest power. Humanity's greatest mental strength lies in the power of its thoughts— our actions are rooted in and are driven by our thoughts.

The driving force of thought is emotion, which in a sense represents the feminine side of masculine thought. Many people are challenged both emotionally and mentally. Failure to think things through can lead to incomplete life situations. Thoughts are energies that can exert a challenging, harmful influence if we are not wholly aware of our own thought processes, and therein lies the danger. We can lose ourselves and be overwhelmed by the intellectual and emotional mindsets of those around us. We require all our concentration to stick to our personal path and avoid losing our way. This is precisely why you should pay close attention to your own thoughts, so that you can recognize where you have not thought things through and identify any incomplete thinking that is not conclusive.

Your thoughts trigger and affect situations, so there are as many options and possibilities as there are people on Earth, but the end goal is the same for everyone. Each soul is on its way back, returning to a unity that cannot be described in words. Personal self-determination affects the length of this journey, which lies solely within the power of the individual. You can progress in life through your thoughts, which provide the impetus for their own completion. Once you have a thought about something, destiny has already embarked upon its path. Every thought releases—or indeed steals—energy. Test this out right now by thinking about someone you love, and then feel how invigorated and full of energy you feel. Now think of someone whose behavior you dislike, and see how tired, depleted, and weak you feel. It is your inner attitude that strengthens or weakens you.

When we are very angry with someone, it is not that we are angry at that person but rather that we are unwilling to recognize and accept the unpleasant aspects of ourselves manifested through the presence of this person. We become annoyed at ourselves because we are giving the other person so much power by paying attention to the way they are and becoming distracted from ourselves. We do not like to be reminded of our weaknesses, but this process offers an opportunity to find true and real freedom. The cosmic law is as follows:

> **Every** thought comes true eventually. Life makes no distinction between good and evil, or between positive or negative; it does not judge but allows every experience.

You have the power to change your current situation and steer it in a new direction. The power of the mind is wasted by those who use it to instead obstruct and avoid situations. Their first thought is about what they will not be doing and how to preempt potential questions. Many people only ever know what they do not want, which then blinds them to what they could have. Thought offers an opportunity to create situations, however, and now is the ideal moment to give your life a fresh steer toward actual happiness. Offer yourself this chance.

Stop telling yourself that you are unable to change anything, and instead start changing the things that can be changed today. Think about the way you approach those around you and do so with a different mindset. You will be amazed at the results that this change can deliver. Smile, and the world smiles with you. Give yourself the opportunity and strength to change things, precisely by being aware that you really do have the power to change everything, and allow happiness and fulfillment to enrich your life. Your abilities and strengths will grow through your own conscious attitude and you will find it easier to achieve your true goals.

You can make the impossible possible! Allow this truth to take root in your mind and it will start to work its magic. Be very conscious of yourself and your attitudes. This is the key to achieving useful and liberating insights. Keep your focus on the way you are thinking: which of your thoughts originated with you and which have you adopted from others? Are you thinking ahead to the future or back to the past? This will help you to see if you are growing and progressing or regressing.

How to Master Being Human

Life is an apprenticeship, during the course of which we all repeatedly come up against our own selves. We are here to know ourselves and to follow our paths. Each moment is an opportunity to free ourselve of negativity through a conscious change to our attitudes. "I am what I am, and I am what reveals itself again and again in every encounter and relationship."

We may try to "get out of our own way" and yet still manage to stumble over hurdles and obstacles of our own making, whether spiritual, mental, or emotional. We are suffering from ourselves, so to speak, and yet we must all live with ourselves, even if we are in conflict with our very selves, as many of us are, having failed to grasp that the cause of everything we encounter lies within us. If we see ourselves as our own worst enemy, life will appear hostile and threatening. It is difficult to develop greatness and generosity of spirit if we lack self-worth. How can we give if we feel we have nothing to give? Always remember that people become winners—and indeed losers—through themselves. We are all both our own problem and our own solution.

Repeated rejection of oneself creates an unhealthy and unsatisfactory mindset, whereas challenging situations allows people to appreciate themselves again, to discover a new direction in which to channel their strengths. Paralysis, for example, triggers a longing and then a desire for movement. People place limitations on or free themselves according to what they consider possible. Our horizons are determined by our aspirations. What are you more likely to do? Tell yourself that you cannot do something, or declare that you are now ready for all the best and highest achievements in life? The choice is yours. What we see in others is what we are ourselves. We tend to accept and manifest this. The things we fear are the things we have long since set in motion. The things we think are the things that will come true. Life does not distinguish between good and evil, or positive and negative. You will experience what you have thought or "dreamed up." The world is the way that you think it is.

Life views everyone the same way and gives everyone the same opportunities. We have been granted the freedom of being able to think for ourselves, but thought "hygiene" is also essential. Many people are unaware of the power of their thoughts, which means, of course, that ultimately our fears can also become reality. We want to be pleasantly surprised by life and despair when this fails to happen. "I wish things were different from the way I think." However, life is only ever the way we ourselves think it is: the limits of our thoughts are the limits of our lives.

Worrying about what another person might think of us is simply a waste of time. We are wasting energy on proving to someone else that we are not the way they may think we are. Do you have so many worries that you cannot see life for what it is? Are your fears getting the upper hand? People tend to feel weaker, with their strength and vitality depleted, when they focus on what they lack. They can easily imagine having too little or nothing, but they have great difficulty in imagining steady growth. It is challenging to remain focused on your goals and not to allow yourself to be distracted. People presume that others are not thinking about them in a positive way, and as a result are constantly checking whether this is the case. Negative fears cause people to question the good that they encounter and to wonder where the "catch" is. Fears prevent goodness prevailing in the long term. However, do not be afraid. You only have yourself to fear when you stand in the way of your own solution.

Many people fear what other people think and so are constantly seeking to protect themselves. Those who do so fear that others have evil intentions, but by doing so they give others the actual power to harm. Ultimately, protection is of no use to them because they are already imagining harm. They consider others to be at fault and so focus all their attention on monitoring and checking up on these other people. They feel tense all the time and fear the worst, and as a result fail to enjoy life.

We should focus on ourselves and find encouragement in the things that go well for us, our daily victories, however great or small. We will continue to grow. We are here to rediscover our own greatness and to manifest our qualities. Life challenges us to show our true greatness, and we discover this through our mental attitude.

By sharing our values we increase them, but by being constantly divided we create lack and distance ourselves from ultimate happiness. As long as we entertain the thought that we are not good enough, this will become our reality. We are right about what we think. People feel provoked by a word or by couched allusions, and they react angrily to certain statements and actions. In doing so, they show that they have been affected by what someone has said or done. But everything that annoys us is really to do with ourselves. We reveal our dependence and attitudes through our negative responses. We lose control and cease to be aware of what is important or essential. We need to recognize in what circumstances, and how, we react, and to monitor how conscious our responses and actions are. Whenever we feel challenged by the actions of others, we should clarify this relationship and/or encounter.

The solution to achieving and living at the highest level lies within each of us. For example, think about how you feel about a particular future meeting; if you anticipate certain reactions, they are more likely to occur, unless you meet someone who shows you how different things can be. Such moments put our own small-mindedness to shame but at the same time are reminders of our innate capacity for greater things. You can achieve what others achieve. Trust in yourself and your values. It would be much easier to just let things happen, to take a situation as it comes and to act in the moment, or indeed not to act at all.

Ego is, love lives! The evolution of the ego

The woodcarver carves Pinocchio the puppet. He is the creator and Pinocchio his creation, but what happens when the creation suddenly believes he is the creator? He recognizes his limitations but has no wish to accept them. Pinocchio is the ego, as it were, that wishes to decouple itself from the power that created it. The woodcarver is not scared of losing this puppet as he knows he can create new puppets whenever he likes. The puppet is only aware of its own existence and begins to fight for a long life while suspecting that the end will be soon.

Why does Pinocchio lie? Why do people lie? You want to convince people of certain things and to look good in their eyes because you need them and expect from them things that you feel you do not possess yourself. All fear of loss and existential angst is tied to the ego. The ego has a tendency to rip something out of context and then use it to pin down or pressure other people. It is fixated on the reactions of others. Ego reacts to ego. The ego is the part of us that fakes dependence. It is also the small-mindedness that lives within its limits. Consciousness is seeing the whole picture.

Most of humanity suffers from itself. People suffer from prejudices, judging others and yet being unable to move forward themselves. The ego within us has a tendency to recall the weaknesses of others. Unfortunately, many people are more likely to remember the things that others are not good at, and so overlook their positive actions and aspects. By the law of resonance, this then becomes the way they themselves are treated. The ego holds onto what it believes are legitimate accusations to lay at the door of others in order to reprimand them. The ego has been constantly nurtured and developed since birth, with the result that our perspective on feelings, on true love, can remain blocked. Love is always there and will never leave us, but as long as our attention is focused on the ego, we will fail to notice love.

So how does the ego present itself? The ego fixates on receiving affirmations from those around it. It seeks control and power. It focuses on the actions of others and tries to convince us that they, and not we, are in the wrong. This attitude leads to bitter disappointment, however, as it changes nothing. The ego plots revenge; it wants to be needed by other people, to demonstrate power, while at the same time exposing the impotence and dependence of others. "You are nothing without me!" says the ego as it tries to convince others into also believing it, in the hope that they will be intimidated and continue to be at the ego's disposal.

The ego is separation from our own being. From an early age, we are told—and indeed shown—that we depend on other people, and so the ego grows to become a tormenting spirit that makes life challenging and distances us from love. "You are alright. It is just your partner who does everything wrong." The ego is flattered by such assurances, but they change nothing and never lead to a happy and fulfilling relationship. The ego always tries to assure us that others, and not it, should make the first move. This deceitful attitude leaves us unhappily dependent and stuck in a futile rut.

Ego is fixation, dependency, powerlessness, subjugation, a desire for revenge, envy, *schadenfreude*, fear of loss, existential angst, victimhood, doubt, anger, hatred, irreconcilability, judgment, conflict, mental forgetfulness, and all kinds of compulsion. It embodies the obsessive fears associated with survival, which cloud our view of the eternal being of the great mind. The powerful ego keeps people from true love. Our challenge is to master our ego so that the mind of the great Creator that wishes to be manifest through us can assert itself. If we are looking for a holistic solution, we should ask ourselves what love would do and listen to and be guided by our instincts. The ego is generally driven by emotion. Be mindful and take note of when your ego reacts and when your great mind is present; your presence of mind is of the greatest importance.

As long as we cling to judgments, we cannot believe in change and personal growth. Prejudices encourage us to disengage and maintain our distance, and any distance maintained through misguided value judgments prevents such encounters from being enriching. Prejudices reveal inner fear and highlight personal weakness. We fail to give others the chance to reveal how they have changed and grown, revealing just how stuck in our own rut we remain. When we come to a halt while others carry on, this naturally leads to a parting of the ways because sharing in something is no longer possible. If we separate from certain people and situations, we separate from ourselves. We should not plan to have separation or parting in our lives but instead strive for a liberating, loving coexistence. However, be careful: the desire to have and to keep hold of something inevitably results in loss. People stay together as long as they are able to give something to each other. Everything else must ultimately go its separate way, since our personal essence cannot assert itself. Sharing brings increase, more of something.

Difficult though this may be to believe, remember that each person is a divine being that has come to this world of its own volition in order to continue to develop at the highest level. We are here to free ourselves from the shackles of self-imposed dependency and powerlessness, and to experience love. We experience enlightenment when we illuminate the dark shadows of our thoughts.

Every soul chooses its life on Earth to comprehend creation in its actual sense, so it is truly a tragedy to observe how some make life more difficult and place obstacles in their own way. How much easier and more pleasant things would be if we could simply be friendly. How joyful a life free of stress and conflict would be. However, most people consider conflict to be unavoidable, having been taught from an early age that they must put up a fight or be beaten. The downfall they fear becomes their lived experience, and this nurtures hostility and reinforces their expectations of life-threatening situations. We would rather suspect that someone is our enemy than have to rely on their friendship. Enemies surround us and we must protect ourselves. Life becomes hostile to life, as we live in constant fear of the end and overthink. Thoughts can be the root cause of stress and fear.

My thoughts, my power

Are things really how we think they are? Let's shine a light into the darkness of our thoughts. We think too much, we overthink, and most of what we think is wrong. We should try to think less and leave more space for knowing and feeling. Essentially, there is no time, compulsion, or fear. Anything is possible. The roots of limitation lie in thinking. A thought is the figurative imagination of an idea: embark upon a thought and there is an immediate response to it. Thinking also motivates life, and a train of thought leads to a compulsion to take action. A thought will not leave us in peace, will not let us sleep, and drives us toward certain behaviors. It robs us of our peace or, more accurately, hides it from us. Thoughts steer the flow of energy and hold sway over our activity. A thought triggers action and motion or paralyzes movement.

It is always important to think about what motivates us, to ask why we strive for change or desire certain things. If the starting point is a lack of something, the end point will be an even greater lack. It is interesting to observe how people experience an energy shift with the utterance of a few specific words. Their aura (energy field) can collapse instantly, but equally it can be rebuilt with a single word. I carried out an exercise in a seminar, challenging the participants to observe themselves when I said "tax return." It had a detrimental affect on each person's energy field, as they thought back to relevant experiences that they had had. Most reverted to their usual attitudes towards tax, thinking to themselves: "It's so complicated and tedious. I can't do it. I'm so glad I can delegate it to someone else. . . ." It was sad to see that it occurred to no one to think instead that they had a high-earning job, could complete their tax return "standing on their head," were financing an efficient infrastructure with their tax dollars, and so were contributing to the common good.

Rather than rethinking the situation and adopting a new attitude, we try to simply get through, indeed, to survive such unpleasant moments. Life becomes a daily struggle for survival, and we squander our energy on thinking how to protect, prevent, and defend things.

Instead, think about adopting the following, ideal, approach to life:

We use our energy to create situations, so it follows that we are full of vitality and spirit. Instead of thinking, "I cannot do this or that," tell yourself, "I can easily take control of this situation." Say, "Blessed is the power of my mind, which will be evident in everything that I do."

Dare to do everything, and fear nothing. Believe in yourself and apply your strengths to the things that are meant to be instead of squandering your strengths on pointless fears. Avoid losing yourself further in passing judgment but be happy instead at all the insights you have gained. Long live life and your amazing being!

In essence, what truly counts is what we ourselves—not others—think. Of course, we can be inspired and spurred on by other people's thoughts, but unfortunately all too often people allow themselves to be intimidated by gloomy predictions about the future expressed by others.

The future begins with your thoughts today. If someone thinks and fears that their pension, for example, is in danger and begins to imagine in vivid detail that they are being betrayed by the system, then this will be the outcome. Everyone must ultimately take responsibility for the things they manifest in life. Try not to be influenced by the media (radio, television, newspapers, politics, and so on), but think for yourself. If you really want to be happy and rich in blessings, do not leave thinking to others. Individuals are right, not the masses.

Complaining does not deliver solutions but instead simply compounds suffering. Herein lie the roots of how we choose to encounter life. When we complain about unpleasant conditions, we only nurture those very condittions, and our mental energy reinforces and extends their influence. Many people find it easier to adopt a negative stance than to allow positive things to enter their life. We fall into the trap of being too lazy and comfortable to think consciously for ourselves.

It is only when we look at the overall picture that we can grasp its true meaning. Both abundance and lack begin in the mind. We become infected because thinking is a disease that needs to be cured if we do not want to perish from it.

Those who neglect themselves will be sidelined by life

We are primarily responsible to and for ourselves.

We must live with ourselves. Many continue to struggle with this idea and so mentally feed their failure instead of daring to allow themselves better things. Those who define themselves by the attention of others are lost. They await from others the very recognition that they should be giving themselves.

Just Switch!

Many believe this is impossible to do. Some prefer to switch off entirely when they feel they are in a hopeless situation and keep everything at arm's length in a vain attempt to combat their own lack of ability. Many just try to get through things somehow in the hope that time will resolve matters, but they will have to wait a very long time for that to happen. Even when death might seem to bring an to end suffering, each soul will continue to follow its path with its own ingrained attitudes, choosing similarly difficult life situations to overcome.

People remain who they are, in a self-determined sense. Waiting simply demonstrates fear of the future. Those who wait miss opportunities in the present. What are we waiting for? We are the ones who will create a better world, not some other power. Every single moment is the right time to make a start on something new. Those who procrastinate will never start anything. Are you prone to saying that you will do certain things "one day?" The future remains the future. Instead, try saying, "I can really imagine doing it right now."

Just one word is enough

A single word is enough to lift or depress a person's mood. Each word is a channel that guides the relevant energy into our existence. Our thoughts are formed and expressed in words and betray our inner attitudes.

The right word at the right time can bring about fundamental change. People who get bogged down in a stream of words often fail to explain things properly. Each attempt at explanation indicates seeking approval due to a lack of self-confidence. In addition, people who always say the same thing reveal long-held attitudes. One targeted word is generally more effective than an endless stream; a single word provides food for thought.

Some words exert a powerful influence on the subconscious by prompting activity. These (switch)words influence our basic attitudes and help our minds to escape from the ruts in which they have become stuck. They can also help us to enjoy pleasant and enriching experiences. A word hangs in space, so to speak, and challenges our attitudes. The key is to act in the present, in the here and now that holds the power for change. Use switchwords when a shift in attitude is required.

A personal recommendation: Do seemingly insurmountable attitudes constantly trip you up? Do you only ever grasp the real meaning of what you've said only once you have said it? Do you simply have nothing left to say on negative occasions? Do you often find yourself provoked into saying something before you have really had the time to think things through properly?

Make your life much easier by writing out some of the words and phrases in this book and posting them on something that you walk past on a daily basis (your refrigerator door, desk, or cupboard). They will act as a constant reminder. Things will become easier, and those around you will also benefit. A word hangs in space, literally, and influences the energy of all those present.

We Already Have All the Answers

We are already equipped at birth with the solutions we need for the various challenges that life brings. During spiritual life-planning before birth, the soul chooses the conditions and situations it wants to master, bringing with it all the necessary answers. Since life's solutions lie in actions, people forget this knowledge when they enter the limited world of form and thought. Nor is there any point in having knowledge of something in advance, since each moment in the present can be experienced consciously. Otherwise you would only be waiting for certain encounters in the future and would not live consciously in the present. If you fail to live consciously in the present, no future event will bring happiness. You determine in this moment how something will continue to be in your life. How you view life will come to pass.

I had an important encounter with my inner world at the age of sixteen. I knew that a return to my inner knowledge would resolve everything, so I did all in my power to see things clearly once more. However, my inner friends were saying: "It's not the right time for you to know. Only once you have mastered certain situations and recognized yourself fully within them, and have taken responsibility for all your shortcomings and ceased to blame other people for your life, only then will we show you everything. You will find out what it all means." The moment I was shown everything occurred when I was forty-five years old. So what happened? I no longer wished to carry on living in this form, so strong was the yearning to live forever in this indescribable warmth, love, and boundlessness. This earthly world seemed so

trivial to me, even though I have always enjoyed different free-
doms and have always been blessed with optimism. My friends
said: "It would be the same for everyone. You would only want to
go home. However, it is very important to be in this world and to
see and live out what you have to do. Had you known 'that,' you
wouldn't have wanted to live 'this' anymore, and although you
had this knowledge from the beginning, it must be converted into
actions and deeds."

Knowledge always serves the moment and spurs us into action in and
from this moment. All learning is the soul re-remembering. However,
those who fail to apply knowledge are ensnared in their own thoughts,
caught up in the theory. Knowledge frees us.

We all have opportunity within us, available at any time, but since
most people live in conflict, the path to a solution can appear blocked.
Doubt reinforces separation and obstructs solutions, such as when we
find ourselves torn in different directions, unable to choose which path
to take. Although emotion points us toward resolutions, knowledge, and
holistic understanding, reason, on the other hand, feeds on doubt and
anticipates difficulties, thereby activating the thinking process. This is
the constant struggle between emotion and reason. Reason needs to be
busy and employed, whereas emotion is revealed in quietness. Emotion
shows the way to true knowledge and holistic understanding. If we look
at only a part of a given situation, it may seen incomprehensible. The
solution lies in looking at the solution as a whole, holistically. If thought
gains the upper hand, emotion is suppressed, intensifying our feelings
of stress and division. When we think, we are essentially wholly absent.

Using the analogy of an organization or company, emotion (let's
call it the subconscious) can be said to represent the company's skilled
workforce, therefore the subconscious represents the skills that are
available. Expert workers are also part of the company, who can find a
solution for every eventuality. Reason or deliberate control (let's call it
daily consciousness) is the CEO, who is supposed to act on the recommendations of the company. However, in most cases, the chief executive

works against the company and makes decisions without listening to the expert advice of the staff. The CEO acquires information from outside the company and operates according to this rather than in accordance with the available options.

When a CEO is not sufficiently interested in their own company and capable staff, they measure themselves against other organizations and seek to push things through for which their own company lacks the basic requirements, simply because other basics are available. Due to a lack of awareness of our own potiential, we often use our strengths incorrectly or even ignore them. After a while, a company's workforce decides to withhold its labor since taking loss after loss is no fun, and it is even less fun when experts cannot bring their own skill and knowledge to bear. The subconscious (the company), stands for solutions and profit, but reason is in charge of everything. In fact, all a chief executive needs to know is that they have capable staff. The CEO is responsible for the company's profit and survival and should target and coordinate the efforts of the staff. However, if the CEO were to work with the company, the whole enterprise would flourish. Everyone would share their insights and grow from their experiences, and the profit would grow, too. You do not need to *think* the solution, you only have to *want* it! If you find yourself in a difficult situation, just say CHANGE.

Certain code words are available to bring a CEO and company back into alignment, commanding the subconscious to take immediate action and find a solution. Chief executives give an order because they have complete faith in their company's strengths and are aware of its full potential. The company then tries its utmost and genuine miracles can be the result.

You will be amazed at how a single word can change your inner attitudes and see your inherent strengths take effect.

Anyone, young or old, can give their life new direction and allow themselves greater happiness. Today!

Attitude is infectious and can be transmitted from one person to another, so take the decision right now to see how infectious you can be in this world. We can create paradise together.

How to Use Switchwords

It is important to approach using switchwords in the right way. For example, do not simply say your chosen switchword out loud and then sit back and wait for something amazing to happen. This will undermine the switchword's effects. Be guided by your intuition, but do not give up if the word fails to have the required effect the first time you use it. Miracles will happen. If it seems as though everything around you is in disarray, a single word will probably be sufficient to restore order. However, if you yourself are the problem, you will have to use the code word more frequently until you are able to change your attitude and emerge from the mental rut in which you have become stuck. It will be well worth the effort. You will feel increasingly at ease as time goes by because life can now share all its best qualities with you. And you yourself are worth so much once more.

The message the New Age brings is as follows:

We are uniting in consciousness of our qualities

Do not focus on shortcomings but instead on existing qualities, which will reward you by bearing fruit and bringing you endless and enriching rewards.

The use of switchwords is the combining of existing strengths in conscious unity.

It is not necessary to keep to the rhythms or the number of repetitions of the switchwords suggested in this book (4 x 7 for TOGETHER, for example). They are merely recommendations. However, the repetition of the switchwords will form a kind of melody if you take a breath whenever two asterisks (**) are indicated. They will be just as effective if you decide not to do so, but breathing allows the divine life energy to flow and experience plays a part. You can say the switchword just once, and without any particular emphasis, or whisper it, or simply say it to yourself. But do say it aloud, do not just think it.

It is also possible to combine switchwords if you wish. Your subconscious will decide what is best in the moment. Always remember that you are the CEO, so you are the one who must give the order to take action, therefore you must be present at all times. You must always be there to lead and guide. You are the one who decides and chooses the future of your own company, in other words, your life, and what profits you can generate.

Please note: DO NOT THINK the solution, you should simply want it!

To illustrate this point, a man was caught in a traffic jam and remembered his girlfriend's advice to use the switchword ONWARD on such occasions. He said TRAFFIC ONWARD and was surprised when the line of cars became even longer, with even more cars joining it.

Why did this happen? A single word (ONWARD) would have been sufficient.

The effect will be even more powerful if you say the switchword while pressing your index finger, middle finger, and thumb together, as if you were sprinkling spice on your food. This gesture concentrates energy and makes you more effective. You hold your own happiness in your own hands, quite literally. Miracles can take place through you, and you make your own reality real.

You are fully responsible for and are in total charge of your office, namely your own great personality. That you exist is already the greatest miracle, and more miracles in this reality will come to pass through you. Always assume the greatest power; you are power, life, and love.

If we strive for a solution, love will lead us

Please note: Allowing any doubts to creep in will hamper your hard work and progress, leaving room for setbacks. So as soon as even the slightest doubt raises its head, just say CHANGE.

Using switchwords every day: Be aware of the opportunities that are open to you. If you are looking for the right word for a particular situation or challenge, or just for the day itself, open this book and allow your intuition to guide you to the word that will shift your attitude, enabling your wish to be fulfilled to the maximum and most positive effect. Experiment. Switch according to your gut feeling. It is impossible to do something wrong, the wrong thing would be not to do it at all.

THE SWITCHWORDS

A Dictionary of Switchwords

How to Use the Switchwords

Read the switchword lists across the page from left to right, saying the words aloud or repeating them in your mind (see p. 30).

For each switchword, you will see a suggestion for the number of repetitions to use, along with instructions on when to take a breathing pause (indicated by two asterisks **). These are merely recommendations, and you are of course free to choose your own rhythm and number of repetitions.

Repeating the switchwords will allow you to visualize "in your mind's eye" how the switchword will work. The repetitions create a rhythm that amplifies the power of the word.

TOGETHER

Say TOGETHER twenty-eight times in a row.
Take a breathing pause where indicated (**).

together	together	together	together	together
together	together	**		
together	together	together	together	together
together	together	**		
together	together	together	together	together
together	together	**		
together	together	together	together	together
together	together			

TOGETHER combines those things that bring completion. Only what is complete makes sense.

When the ego is too heavily involved, the danger is that you will focus on a single detail in an entire situation or set of circumstances and make this a stumbling block. You could end up spending too much time concentrating on this detail, exhausting yourself while becoming a burden on those around you. TOGETHER promotes a view of the whole context. When someone cannot remember a past event, it is often due to a deception of the ego. The ego concentrates on the deeds of others, placing less emphasis on personal responsibility. If people come to my consulting room hoping to resolve a conflict in their partnership or some other aspect of their life together, I ask them specifically for real examples of situations they have experienced. I ask questions, and when the person seeking help tells me that they can't remember exactly, I know that we are dealing with a blanket apportioning of blame. People who observe themselves with honesty in such situations are close to the actual solution. Nothing happens to us that is not connected with us.

TOGETHER ensures that the subconscious is fully cooperative with the superconscious once more. It brings about alignment and integration and encourages a consistent approach. The two separated SELVES are reunited so that together they achieve the highest and the best of things. TOGETHER releases feelings of division and activates the essential union of the highest forces.

TOGETHER cannot unite people or things that are incapable of a holistic combination. It cannot be employed as a tool for manipulation, for example, but it can support the potential union of appropriate things. TOGETHER clarifies if things actually do belong together. If this is not the case, stop trying to bring them together and do not waste any more time or effort.

To achieve the best results, say your first name and TOGETHER out loud in the morning; you will be surprised at just how positively your skills and attributes come into their own on a holistic level. Promote a feeling of team spirit in your daily interactions with others by using TOGETHER. If you find that you cannot concentrate and are becoming too easily distracted, TOGETHER will help you to apply your seven senses more effectively. If you find you are missing a final piece of a puzzle, say "project TOGETHER," and just see how everything miraculously falls into place.

Would you like to awaken your clairvoyant powers? If so, try asking questions about a partnership. For example, say "Adam and Eve TOGETHER" and listen to what your gut feeling tells you. If these two people do not really belong together, there will be a strong indication of this, and/or your feelings will tell you how likely they are to remain in a partnership. If you want to check your own relationship, say your own first name and that of your partner, and then say TOGETHER twenty-eight times.

If long-term holistic happiness is impossible, you will be able to recognize this without judgment and then to let go. You always have a choice: you can compromise and stay together, or take a chance on absolute love, and trust that life will always want the highest and best for you. TOGETHER is the master key that aligns everything so that true fulfillment can be experienced.

AHEAD

Say AHEAD eleven times in a row.

ahead	ahead	ahead	ahead
ahead	ahead	ahead	ahead
ahead	ahead	ahead	

Have you lost touch with yourself? Are you wondering what a particular person thinks of you at this very moment and are feeling self-conscious as a result? Does it make you feel stressed to be unable to focus your thoughts on yourself? Use the magic word AHEAD. Say your first name and then AHEAD eleven times. Your essence will return to the fore, and you will be recognized as an individual with your own desires and expectations. Repeat the procedure every time your thoughts stray and you feel as though you have wandered away from yourself. Make sure to get yourself AHEAD! You are a top priority. Stop putting yourself in the shadow of those around you. Shadows cannot expect happiness and fulfillment

Do you feel as though you are always taking one step ahead and two steps back, and that your needs are always last in line? AHEAD is an ideal switchword to change these circumstances.

Are you falling behind with your plans? Are you keen to take the lead once more? AHEAD will help you to achieve this. Similarly, if you are running late and want to make up lost time, simply say AHEAD. If you are behind with work, a particular project, or some kind of race or competition and want to pick up the pace, say AHEAD. If you are stuck in a line that is not moving, again use AHEAD. Perhaps your team is losing and you want to mobilize additional strength to regain the lead? You will get ahead more quickly with TOGETHER and AHEAD, and always in a healthy and balanced way.

Here's an example to illustrate this. A man wanted to surprise his wife with a trip to a special concert, but the show was very popular and he had forgotten to order tickets in time. Nevertheless, he went to the booking office, equipped with his inner confidence and his "GET two of the best tickets for the x performance" attitude. There were already two lines of people waiting for tickets. His inner voice advised him to stand in the line to the right, although it did not appear to be making any progress. His reason was telling him that perhaps he should stand in the other line, which was moving more quickly, but his feelings were telling him to stay where he was and say AHEAD. The man did not give in to his doubts and trusted in his chosen solution. Suddenly, someone emerged from the auditorium and came directly up to him, saying, "I have two spare tickets. You can have them if you would like them." The man was delighted as they were two of the best seats. He was very pleased that he had kept to his decision successfully, and his enjoyment of the concert with his wife was all the greater because of it.

BACK

Say BACK ten times in a row.

back   back   back   back   back
back   back   back   back   back

Have you missed an important moment? Do you sometimes wish for a second chance to do something? If so, simply say "Situation x BACK."

To illustrate this, here's a short story. My friend and her acquaintance were on a trip to a neighboring country for Christmas shopping. They made several purchases and took the train home, hoping to get the export invoices stamped during the train ride so that they could reclaim the sales tax. They were having a lively conversation, but just before the border they were shocked to realize that they had missed the customs official. However, my friend calmed her companion down, telling her not to worry and that he would come back again. She said, "Customs official, BACK!" Her companion was initially skeptical but was then astounded when the customs official came running toward them. My friend immediately stopped him to get their papers stamped. The official said, "You're lucky. I never usually come back, but today I had a feeling I had forgotten something at the front of the train." He also stamped the papers of some of the other passengers in the carriage; they were delighted at his return because they too had missed him when he came through. This small miracle was not only a help to but pleased many.

You cannot turn back time, but you can get missed opportunities BACK. However, it is always best to be attentive in the present to avoid having to say AHEAD and BACK too many times.

SETTLE

Say SETTLE sixteen times in a row.
Take a breathing pause where indicated (***).

settle	settle	settle	settle	**
settle	settle	settle	settle	**
settle	settle	settle	settle	**
settle	settle	settle	settle	

The cosmic order determines all the processes in the universe. The laws of life are at work. Does order need restoring? Have things gone off the rails? Is there a misunderstanding or are you tormented by thinking about some unfinished business?

SETTLE restores order to your world. SETTLE will bring the cosmic law of balance to bear.

There is a natural order in universal togetherness, but things can be knocked off course through incorrect behavior or the unequal shouldering of a burden. The switchword SETTLE restores balance to disrupted processes. If the functioning of one of the body's organs (or indeed the entire body) has been upset, for example, this word can help it to return to normality. It will of course take time, so be patient. Have you stepped on the toes of a friend or acquaintance, metaphorically speaking, and are now obliged to apologize? Are you unsure of how to restore order to a complicated situation? Do you feel compelled to do something or placed under pressure by a particular organization or set of circumstances?

Simply say:

SETTLE financial matter
SETTLE blood pressure
SETTLE cardiac function

SETTLE bladder function
SETTLE the relationship between Adam and Eve
SETTLE the matter of xyz
SETTLE inheritance
SETTLE contractual details
SETTLE life
SETTLE family affair

COMPLIMENT

Say the word COMPLIMENT twelve times in a row.
Take a breathing pause where indicated (**).

compliment	compliment	compliment	compliment	**
compliment	compliment	compliment	compliment	**
compliment	compliment	compliment	compliment	

In the truest sense, making a mistake is punishing oneself for an inability to concentrate fully or effectively. An error is, so to speak, when essential parts of the whole have erred. If we concentrate on what has erred, we will only see mistakes. Fear of inappropriate behavior can paralyze us, robbing us of any pleasure that we would otherwise take from what we do.

Are you always frightened of making mistakes? Do you regret some of your past actions? Are you constantly checking up to see whether your partner or your child has done something wrong? Do you always expect people to make mistakes? Blaming someone for a supposed mistake is punishing yourself because you fear having to suffer the consequences of that person's mistake. None of us are keen to be reduced to our past mistakes. Those who reduce others and/or themselves to their past mistakes are depriving others and themselves of the chance to find holistic fulfillment. A mental fixation on mistakes makes us commit the worst mistakes ourselves.

Instead of harboring regrets, try to acknowledge the inner attitudes that have led to certain situations. You now have sufficient wisdom to recognize and admit the limitations of your past attitudes. You should be very happy that this will allow you to assert more of your true greatness. Nothing can be undone, but things can be changed, and now, thanks to your experiences, you will be able to act with greater wisdom and more effecively. We only learn from our mistakes when we store them in our memory as holistic experiences and not as mistakes. Insight into a particular situation's outcome enriches and liberates us, once we know how things are. People who live in constant fear of making a mistake are ensnared in the judgment of others. Dependence upon the decisions and praise of others compels us to try to please all the time. Those afraid of making mistakes will nevertheless commit them precisely because they are frightened of doing so.

Blaming others reveals an enslavement to the ego. Instead of saying, "I have to suffer because of your mistakes," ask, "Is everything okay? Have I taken care of everything?" This will allow your subconscious to highlight situations where things may not be quite right. Compliment and appreciate your child, activating his or her strength, and you will achieve the greatest happiness. The people who recognize greatness in others are on the path to greatness themselves.

> COMPLIMENT the health of my/your body
> COMPLIMENT the beauty of my body, which has made my very existence possible, and may I derive joy from its function and form every day
> COMPLIMENT my surroundings
> COMPLIMENT the work I am doing today
> COMPLIMENT the cleansing powers and effects of this water
> COMPLIMENT my masterful being
> COMPLIMENT the miracle of life
> COMPLIMENT the actions of x
> COMPLIMENT my ability
> COMPLIMENT the growth and force of Nature
> COMPLIMENT the company of x
> COMPLIMENT brings blessings upon actions
> COMPLIMENT activates the courage to attempt anything

ADMIRE

Say ADMIRE eleven times in a row.
Take a breathing pause where indicated (**).

admire	admire	admire	**
admire	admire	admire	**
admire	admire	admire	**
admire	admire		

"How wonderful is that!" "I admire you because you embody the things that I don't dare to do myself!" The things you see, appreciate, and admire in others will one day bring you admiration. To admire something, however, you must first regard it in a relaxed or dispassionate way; any tension is a sign of fear and control that can hamper an objective view. ADMIRE is the magic word that puts the powerful ego back in its box and allows true vision and love to play their part instead.

Ask yourself why you admire a particular person. The answer will reveal the essence of what deserves admiration. The ego seeks its own confirmation and demands admiration from those around it. If it fails to receive this, the ego plots revenge and retaliation, waiting for an opportunity to deny appreciation to others. The outcome is a struggle that distracts from your own core and leads to unnecessary conflict in relationships. You cannot live with someone, but you cannot live without them either. "If you loved me, you would do this (or that) for me!" is a classic statement from an ego in search of external affirmation, convinced that responsibility for mistakes lies elsewhere. The ego triumphs when it convinces others of its own opinion. The ego lives on fear, love lives on trust. You will always encounter resistance if you have an egotistical attitude.

To get rid of all prejudice, say "ADMIRE (name)." To overcome criticism and whenever hostility or a negative attitude creeps in, say "ADMIRE x." The switchword ADMIRE enables you to become aware of the things in life that deserve admiration. You will be admired for your ability to distinguish genuine values. Your approach to life and people will be admirable. ADMIRE will highlight just how worthy you are of admiration. If you have difficulty seeing the good in someone, get rid of this inner reluctance by saying ADMIRE (followed by that person's name). We are all life's miracle, but not all of us are yet ready to recognize that miracle.

NOTICE

Say NOTICE seven times in a row.

notice   notice   notice   notice
notice   notice   notice

Is something or someone in your life worthy of attention or notice? Do you consider it worthwhile to remember things that are remarkable or out of the ordinary? Would you like to be one of these remarkable people yourself? So many people, creatures, things, and deeds are noteworthy, and yet so often they go entirely unremarked. If you think an event is "unusual," or you find someone "extraordinary," make a conscious effort to pay attention to them. They want to reveal miracles to you. If you note a remarkable deed or action, ensure that you will remember it with the word NOTICE.

Unfortunately, we all too often say, "I won't forget that in a hurry," a statement that is in fact a threat from the ego. We might remark that someone we know never notices anything, but why do we say this? Is it because we notice so little ourelves? The ego notices what is missing, the gaps in something; love notices the whole.

If you would like people to notice you in the most positive ways, resolve today to start noticing the positive and constructive actions of others. Your own personal growth will be noticed and people will remark on your unique presence. "I noticed you and I remembered what you said!" Do you still take note of what is important in your life? NOTICE will increase your attention to noteworthy details and bring important insights. Say, "I can now notice the essence!" Use NOTICE and you make a choice; you will notice what is truly important and liberating. Are you confused by irrelevant information that means you fail to notice what is actually going on? When reading a contract, are you keen to identify the important details? Say NOTICE and you will recognize what is meaningful and essential. If someone praises you or you experience something wonderful, fix this permanently in your consciousness by saying NOTICE. If you feel your presence is worthy of notice, say your first name and then say NOTICE seven times. Believe me, people will NOTICE your existence.

CANCEL

Say CANCEL twenty times in a row.
Take a breathing pause where indicated (**).

cancel	cancel	cancel	cancel	**
cancel	cancel	cancel	cancel	**
cancel	cancel	cancel	cancel	**
cancel	cancel	cancel	cancel	**
cancel	cancel	cancel	cancel	

Unnecessary thoughts divert and distract us. Once a thought has formed in our mind, it will take its course. Every thought seeks its realization and is sustained by constant repetition. Thoughts can tease and torment us, and the destructive power of negative thoughts is hard to counteract. They steal sleep and rob us of positivity. They eat up the energy we need to shape our life. Like an alien invader that is beyond our control and wants to manifest in the real world, a negative thought penetrates our peace. Have you ever tried not to think of something or someone? Has a persistent thought loop caused you real suffering? To retract an unpleasant thought, use the magic word CANCEL.

This switchword interrupts thought processes and reveals a way out of situations that have begun badly. Do you sometimes feel that you would like to turn back the clock and undo certain statements or past events, CANCEL can help to mitigate matters. Do you suffer from negative preconceptions instilled in childhood? As soon as a negative train of thought begins, say CANCEL and stop it in its tracks!

TINY

Say TINY five times in a row.

tiny   tiny   tiny   tiny   tiny

TINY promotes courtesy within ourselves and reminds us of our own greatness, while at the same time prompting essential recognition of the greatness of those to whom we are speaking.

Have you lost the sense of your own greatness? Do you feel small and insignificant? Do you sense that others view you with pity? Are you plagued by the thought that you have nothing to say or indeed offer? Have you disempowered yourself by thinking you are nothing and can achieve nothing. Has someone told you this in the past? TINY activates your personal greatness and gives permission for your own splendor.

Do you tend to look down on others and pity them, being capable only of seeing their weaknesses? Does someone still have the power to annoy you, or do you fly into a rage in the presence of some people, responding with anger to certain words or attitudes that offend you? Just say TINY, and you'll be surprised. Your nemesis may become your greatest ally! Use TINY and you will win admirers and inspire enthusiasm in people as your inner magnificence is revealed.

The highest goal of each of us is to achieve our own greatness, and those who recognize greatness in others will be raised to the greatest heights. Those who recognize that others are divine creations are themselves divine. The greatness of every creature, person, animal, and being is worthy of recognition. Those who are generous in their thinking can achieve great things.

ACHIEVE

Say ACHIEVE nine times in a row.
Take a breathing pause where indicated (**).

achieve	achieve	achieve	**
achieve	achieve	achieve	**
achieve	achieve	achieve	

Challenges are always at their greatest just before the finish line, or so people think. Are you scared of not achieving your goal and fearful that your strength will fail you? Are you plagued by the idea that all your efforts could be thwarted? Do you fear you will betray yourself by not being faithful to your plans? Many suffer from fear of failure and harbor doubts that they can achieve what they set out to do. Most people are incarnated only because they did not achieve their life projects in their past life: "Hopefully, I will still be able to experience 'it'!"

ACHIEVE enables you to accomplish everything in your life plan. Use it to mobilize your hidden powers. It will guarantee that you realize your ambitions. Say, "ACHIEVE life goal" and you will be guided and led by destiny. The destination is clear, but the path leading to it is often obscured. We are guided when we want to be led, and talk of happy coincidence when things happen that fulfill and please us. "ACHIEVE life partnership" activates a convergence with the love of your life. However, if a lack of self-love makes you your own worst enemy, true love will take time. To activate your ability to love yourself, say, "ACHIEVE the capacity for love." If you want to win the jackpot in the lottery, for example, try saying "ACHIEVE lottery jackpot," but remember, life will not deliver monetary riches if you neglect your obligations or avoid confronting your weaknesses. The more you cultivate your inner values, the more likely they will be joined by external equivalents. "ACHIEVE the role of . . ." will elevate you to a long-desired office.

Now decide what you wish to ACHIEVE for yourself.

BE

Say BE seven times in a row.

be be be be be be be

Do you feel ill at ease in certain situations? Perhaps you have just one thought in your head: "Get me out of here!" Can you no longer bear to be in the same room as certain people? Do those around you crowd your personal space, leaving no room for you? Are you always looking for escape routes? Are you running away from your reality? BE enables you to be present with your own strength. Is your presence no longer making a mark? Are you sinking silently, without a word of complaint? BE will help you to bring out the key elements of your personality and fill any room with your presence. BE also ensures you leave your mark even when you are silent. Stay, do not run away. BE reinforces your essential presence in the here and now. Recognize your "BE this way/a certain way" for what it is!

BE (rather than the future "will be") delivers progress. If you are still using the expression "I will (do/be such and such)," you are living in the future, and it will never become the present. You might say things like, "I never wanted to become what I am now." People who do not want to become something have already had an inner encounter with their "BE this way/BE a certain way," and so become the very thing they feared.

"Nothing will ever become of you." Without a clear and conscious understanding of BE, people can never achieve their dreams. "I want to BE . . ." is a conscious formulation that allows you to make all your wishes come true. "One day, I'm going to be . . ." will also achieve this, but if you are thinking it now, try to make it come true now, in the present moment. Do not put off happiness until later.

Be omnipresent with BE!

OFF

Say OFF twice in a row.

off   off

Use OFF to turn or break something off to ensure that you are no longer out of kilter or off-balance.

Would you like to cut someone or something off from your life? Would you like to get rid of an old habit? OFF severs old ties, finally freeing you to explore new relationships. Do you always manage to get everything off your chest? Is someone completely fixated on you and cannot shake their obsession? This is where old ties and fixations can be a hindrance, preventing current encounters from taking hold and becoming established. To get rid of something specific, say OFF. It is the magic word that works like a pair of mental scissors. OFF and ONWARD will guide you onto new paths.

AWAY

Say AWAY sixteen times in a row.
Take a breathing pause where indicated (**).

away	away	away	away	**
away	away	away	away	**
away	away	away	away	**
away	away	away	away	

If someone is getting in your way, physically, mentally, or even spiritually, the small switchword AWAY will help. Is a situation or a physical condition weighing you down? Do you want to be free of it and feel better? AWAY will show you how and help you to shoo it away. To get something specific out of your way, AWAY can truly work miracles.

Say, for example:

> Corns AWAY
> Wart AWAY
> Skin blemishes AWAY
> Wrinkles AWAY
> Faulty thinking AWAY
> Anger AWAY . . .

However, what you cannot do is send certain unpleasant people AWAY, out of your life. Those who are still able to annoy you are, in fact, your best friends because they are showing you where more of your own greatness is required. "Love your enemies" in effect means "Love and think of yourself as an almighty being."

AWAY clears the way ahead and allows unlimited access to everything.

SOLVE

Say SOLVE four times in a row.

solve   solve   solve   solve

"First, he was very confused and puzzled, and then he came up with the solution." Things are sometimes so tangled up and knotted in life that it is difficult to distinguish the beginning from the end. Imagine that you tied a knot in a rope and you now want to undo it. You begin with the end nearest to you and work your way back to the start. It is just the same in life, metaphorically speaking: the solution begins in the present and leads back to the beginning of everything. Say the word SOLVE and demonstrate your genuine desire to discover the true solution.

SOLVE activates a solution and eases any situations that have become blocked and frozen. Those who ask for solutions will receive holistic insights. Reaching solutions always entails understanding and realization in the fullest sense, so do not seek the cause of a set of circumstances or you will be heading off down a blind alley that will leave you none the wiser in the end. Those who are looking for causes are often looking to apportion blame, but those who instead strive for solutions are able to recognize cause and effect without passing judgment. Life does not judge but eventually works itself out in our best interests until we have a change of heart. If you are ready for a solution, now is the time to start.

In the case of unpleasant relationships in which battlelines have effectively been drawn up, say "SOLVE association and situation with x." We sometimes overlook details that we have never considered important, but a minor irritation may eventually turn into a major annoyance that is then much more difficult to overcome. From now on, be aware that small things are important but not necessarily serious. Everything changes and everything is eventually resolved, but only you will determine when that time may be. Simply say:

SOLVE problem x
SOLVE guilt
SOLVE money issue x
SOLVE unemployment

SOLVE frees us from our chains and enables the road ahead, our destiny, to be smooth. We are here to disSOLVE the bonds that tie us to old burdens and obligations. Allow yourself to activate the solution NOW.

OH/HO/OHA/OHO

Do you experience tension? Does overthinking and pointless analysis prevent you from adopting a more relaxed view of things? Do undefinable fears make it hard for you to enjoy even the good times? Are you always on edge? Do you feel tense and lack the space in which to develop freely? Do you have little room for maneuver? Are you lacking room to breathe properly in the most profound sense? Sigh and simultaneously say the word OH, and you will immediately feel more relaxed.

OH is the magic word that brings instant calm and relief. When you say this word, you breathe out automatically, immediately creating space. Breathing out frees you for the new direction you need to take. OH helps us to put anxieties aside. Many people suffer from tension because they are always taking things on and letting nothing go. The rhythmn of give and take is disrupted, leading to obstacles and blockages. However, remember that those who give can also take away. OH is synonymous with, "I see you and me in the same light." The outcome is an awareness of what we have in common.

BLUFF

BLUFF dispels fear and helps you to emerge unharmed from threatening situations.

It is important to be aware that fear feeds on time and our imagination, on the mental images that we conjure up, none of which are to do with the present. Everything is good in the present—you fear things that have already happened or, as is more likely to be the case, are yet to take place. Live in the present and use BLUFF to banish unnecessary fears. Fear comes from not knowing and is very different from the sense of heightened awareness that warns us of danger. Fear paralyzes in every respect and seeps into the brain, generally having little to do with the present reality. Films and stories (media, television, newspaper reports . . .) can fill you with fear if you allow yourself to become immersed in such narratives and imagine these same events happening to you in real life. Cleanse your thoughts with the switchword BLUFF, or your unconscious fears may become reality. If you know you are subject to fears and obsessions, start to work with BLUFF, and whenever fear shows its face, press the switchword switch.

> For example, a friend of mine was pushing her bicycle on her way home in the city. A man suddenly ran up to her, ripped her purse out of the pannier, and ran off with it. My friend dropped her bicycle and ran after the thief, asking two men to assist her. The thief suddenly stopped, weapon in hand, but she thought he was only bluffing and was not afraid. They finally let the thief escape after one of the men who had come to her aid said they should back off. My friend then reported the incident to the police, and it was only after the officer told her that the weapon (a pistol) might have been real that she was scared, but not before then. The thief was eventually caught and brought before a judge.

BLUFF frees us from irrational angst and fear.

TRUST

Say TRUST five times in a row.

trust   trust   trust   trust   trust

There is no love without trust.

A lack of trust torments many people and creatures because they are paralyzed by past experiences that remain active in their memory. TRUST is the magic word that paves the way for new experiences that bring progress and embrace new joy. So many people cannot trust those they love. TRUST reactivates awareness of self-love and allows us to be happy and full of confidence once more. Do you trust that life only wants the best for you? By saying TRUST, you are acknowledging the loving providence at work within and behind everything. Say, "I wish to TRUST again, completely and wholeheartedly." This will free you from unnecessary constraints and self-doubt.

Jealousy is a tormenting and evil emotion that prevents true love. So many people suffer from jealousy and are plagued by feelings of inferiority. They find it difficult to imagine that they are really worthy of love, and suspect that their partner intends to betray them, if not today, then sometime in the future.

If trust is destroyed, or you find your own trust shaken, the magic word TRUST will come to the rescue. Trust first in yourself and you will be able to trust anyone and anything while also helping others to gain self-confidence. "I don't trust it!" is an attitude that will be consigned to the past, and should you wish to win the trust of a particular person or creature, the code word TRUST will set this in motion.

ENCOURAGE

Say ENCOURAGE three times in a row.

encourage   encourage   encourage

ENCOURAGE highlights those talents that have been hidden and forgotten and brings them to the fore in the present. "I am encouraging you because I believe in you and recognize your worth." This switchword is of course connected with courage and means that you sense your own hidden potential and are being courageous enough to access it. Life often delivers challenges and expectations that we think we cannot face, but each of these is invariably a gift, within which is an opportunity to express the genius in each of us. Life is a unique challenge that exists in order for us recognize our true greatness once more and to live. The highest existence demands the greatest deeds!

Do you believe you can do so much more? Do you feel that you have never been encouraged in any real sense? Many parents, and indeed teachers, are not fully able to encourage their children or pupils as they have no firsthand experience of being encouraged themselves. How can someone with no self-confidence in any aspect of life encourage others? ENCOURAGE activates the skills with which you entered this world. Be your own encouragement by having the courage to demand everything from life. If you don't ask, you don't get, but if you do ask, you will receive. Nothing is too good for you.

People assailed by doubt when faced with the slightest challenge have never learned to believe in themselves. They diminsh their own strength by believing that they can do nothing. They give up before even starting. "I'm nothing, I can't do anything, and nothing will come of me anyway." You are standing in your own way with this kind of damaging attitude.

Those who remain trapped in this mindset should not be surprised if nothing comes of anything. ENCOURAGE activates those abilities that relate to our personal essence. It expresses individual action, therefore rivals and competitors are no longer relevant, since everyone can make an impact in their own way.

UNDERSTAND

Say UNDERSTAND seven times in a row.

understand   understand   understand   understand
understand   understand   understand

Do you sometimes feel as though you know a great deal but understand nothing? UNDERSTAND is the code word that helps us to turn our knowledge into concrete action. What good is it to have the theory at our disposal and yet achieve nothing in practice? Knowledge that we do not make full use of leaves us with an unpleasant feeling and an inner tension (I must, I should, I know, but . . .).

People who explain things at great length experience a lack in their lives that makes them fear they will not be understood by others. They assume a failure to understand in others that corresponds to their own shortcoming. All too often we hear someone say: "Please just understand what I am trying to say to you." We measure ourselves by our powers of persuasion and often fail to respect the level of knowledge of those we are talking to. UNDERSTAND activates your own comprehension and prompts others to understand more for themselves in order to achieve even greater things with their expanded knowledge.

"Now I finally understand what you were trying to say all those years ago." Our answers and reactions reveal whether we have understood something. Stop fooling yourself by pretending that you have got a handle on everything, while actually understanding nothing. If we understand ourselves and our reality, we uncover a route into the creation of that reality. Many people, however, suffer from a general obtuseness, having been taught from childhood to at least pretend they have understood a fact, even when they have not. Ask questions if you fail to grasp something, but first give yourself a chance by making use of your own knowledge and the insights you have acquired through your own experiences.

Understand yourself as a great being who will take the next step on their journey as soon as the current reality has been fully understood in its entirety. "UNDERSTAND (first name)" will help you to recognize and fully comprehend. It transcends the rational mind; only love is able to understand and grasp the whole. Say UNDERSTAND to activate your all-embracing comprehension.

SEIZE

Say SEIZE twelve times in a row.
Take a breathing pause where indicated (**).

seize	seize	seize	**
seize	seize	seize	**
seize	seize	seize	**
seize	seize	seize	

SEIZE delivers instant possession, giving you everything you have been seeking immediately and guiding you toward it. SEIZE takes you to the exact place where you will find it.

Have you lost or mislaid a particular item? Have you been looking for something for a long time, a pair of shoes or a particular dress? Are you struggling to find a certain word in a particular language? Or perhaps you find yourself saying with increasing frequency, "I know I put it somewhere, I just can't remember where." Just use the word SEIZE and it will reinforce your conviction that you do have the object somewhere and will enable you to find it.

SEIZE car keys
SEIZE soothing lozenges for my throat
SEIZE an apprenticeship in the field of x

There are countless ways to use the magic word SEIZE. Try it yourself and SEIZE those opportunities now.

BEGIN

Say BEGIN eleven times in a row.
Take a breathing pause where indicated (**).

begin	begin	begin	begin	**
begin	begin	begin	begin	**
begin	begin	begin		

Many people simply have no idea where to begin. They start with the very things they know little about, and in so doing place unnecessary obstacles in their own way. Begin with the things that you already know about and can do, and the rest will follow automatically. You will grow with the things you take on.

Some people fail to get started on a project or plan at all because they feel they are not mature enough to do something. Having been told that the first step is the hardest, they avoid new beginnings.

BEGIN will surprise you by revealing just how easy things can be. Now is the time for action and to take the first step on the road to paradise. Start to enjoy your life today, and say:

BEGIN pure pleasure

BEGIN shows you where and how to embark upon something. Everything else will then become far less difficult as you will have overcome your own doubts.

RECOGNIZE

Say RECOGNIZE twenty times in a row.
Take a breathing pause where indicated (**).

recognize	recognize	recognize	recognize	**
recognize	recognize	recognize	recognize	**
recognize	recognize	recognize	recognize	**
recognize	recognize	recognize	recognize	**
recognize	recognize	recognize	recognize	

It can take years, indeed a lifetime, to be able to recognize things for what they really are. Do you sometimes fail to recognize even yourself? There is more to you than you previously thought. RECOGNIZE allows personal memories to rise to the surface, with brutal honesty, and those who are not afraid of confronting their own truth use this switchword to achieve the clarity that in turn prompts great change. Our insights enrich us and make us free. Our readiness to see things as a whole is rooted in our ability to recognize ourselves.

What we consider to be true, or perceive as such, is often limited and one-sided; truth is far more nuanced than perception. As long as we fail to perceive ourselves entirely, we will remain trapped in certain situations, relationships, and processes, still facing the same problems. "What is this situation trying to tell me?" RECOGNIZE guides us toward greater depths of understanding; true freedom lies in genuine self-recognition. "I am a long way from understanding what is essential and grasping the actual meaning." Say RECOGNIZE and your eyes will be open to your true self and you will comprehend all its greatness.

Recognize that you are by far a greater being than the figure you incarnate in this life. True freedom comes with the recognition of what everything is good for. Recognize the real connection with the Source of Creation. Recognize who you truly are by simply using the switchword RECOGNIZE.

BLESS

Say BLESS three times in a row.

bless   bless   bless

BLESS makes wonderful things happen. Blessings fall on and enrich everyone. If this is not yet your own experience, take a look at your attitudes. Do you find everyday life difficult? Do you constantly struggle and still fail to achieve the things that you scarcely dare hope for? BLESS calls upon heavenly powers and activates the higher vibration inherent in all creations. BLESS all that is holy and to be healed. It brings about the highest vibration in every creature. "I BLESS this event" highlights the sublime aspects of a particular moment. Bless the togetherness of a family, business, or project, therefore, and you will see that higher powers are activated.

"Blessed is this driver's journey!" Instead of being angry or irritated by the actions of a motorcycle rider or cyclist who pushes in front of your car at a junction and allowing it to provoke negative thoughts ("They are going to cause an accident"), say:

Blessed is the journey of this rider and blessed is my journey.

You can bless so much, for example:

Blessed is the path I am taking
Blessed is my work
Blessed is my relationship with x
Blessed is the food I eat, which supports my physical health in the most positive way
Blessed is the growth of this plant
Blessed is my existence in the present reality
Blessed is our meeting

Blessed are the actions of our government/president/country
Blessed is the growth of my daughter/my son
Blessed is my prosperity
Blessed is my financial situation
Blessed is my business/project
Blessed are my financial income and expenditure
Blessed is my financial ease
Blessed is the company for which I work
Blessed are the people on their life path
Blessed are my efforts in the matter of x
Blessed is the relationship of x and y
Blessed is my relationship with x
Blessed am I with my gifts
Blessed is the air that we breathe
Blessed is Nature and the Earth, which accompany us in
our existence
Blessed is the Earth and all that it brings forth

BLESS money before you use it so that it can bless other deeds and return to benefit you, multiplied many times over. The blessing of money will make you happy, and those around you will be happy when their involvement is rewarded by the purchases you make. In this way your life will become a true blessing. BLESS brings out the best and the highest. "Blessed is this moment and the gift that you receive right now."

Blessed is your path to come, and every step you take.

STRETCH

Say STRETCH seven times in a row.
Take a breathing pause where indicated (**).

stretch   stretch   stretch   stretch   ******
stretch   stretch   stretch

Are the very best moments in life over far too quickly? Would you like the most enjoyable times to last longer? This is easy to achieve with STRETCH. Learn how to take control of time and simply stretch it out. The switchword STRETCH has an elongating effect.

Say, for example:

STRETCH vacation
STRETCH friendly companionship
STRETCH loving moments
STRETCH the effects of a massage
STRETCH success and profit

STRETCH reinforces and extends pleasure and joy. Just recognizing that a particular moment is wonderful will help to bring other wonderful moments into your life. STRETCH is like an intensive treatment program for positive experiences.

If you have been able to achieve a longstanding goal and would like to enjoy it for longer, use STRETCH. If you would like to extend or prolong a lucrative job or commission, STRETCH will help it to last longer, to the benefit of all concerned.

EXPAND

Say EXPAND six times in a row.
Take a breathing pause where indicated (**).

expand   expand   expand   **
expand   expand   expand

Are you seeking to enhance a particular area of your life? Are you keen to expand your experience of something with which you are already familiar? Are you hoping for some form of external help? For example, to link your company with another to increase your product's market exposure? Would you like to carry on your activities in the same field or sector but feel it is also important to be able to move into new but associated areas? EXPAND will make your existing recipe for success even more nuanced and profitable.

EXPAND enables you to cross existing boundaries and reinforce your influence on cosmic events.

EXPAND allows your personal value to spread into other areas and fields. "Essentially, I would like to EXPAND." This will lead to true growth. Are you ready for it?

MORE

Say MORE fifteen times in a row.
Take a breathing pause where indicated (**).

more	more	more	more	more	**
more	more	more	more	more	**
more	more	more	more	more	

Have you always wanted more and yet always felt there was not enough for everyone? MORE allows us to see more and for more of things to exist. However, be careful when choosing the context in which you use it. Make a very conscious decision about what there should be more of in your life. Before something can be increased and become more, it must already exist or be underway. In other words, you must already have some of whatever it is you want more of, since nothing comes from nothing.

Many things can become more, for example:

MORE recognition
MORE opportunities and options
MORE financial means
MORE personal recognition
MORE talents in the field of x
MORE satisfied customers
MORE financial income
MORE happiness and profit

There is nothing in your way any MORE, apart from you yourself!

TOO!/TOO?

Say TOO once.

too!
or
too?

Have you, too, ever asked what life is all about and what is wanted from you? Did you wait for an answer, or simply let it pass? "You too are involved, so what does it all have to do with you?" This is a good question to ask yourself in terms of taking appropriate responsibility and helping resolve situations caused by others. The situation is the same when you are a bystander at a dispute, when you too are called upon to help resolve things. When a child says "Me too," it is often fobbed off with the answer "Not now," which can lead later to an unhealthy passivity. You may not know why everything affects you too (although nothing happens in our reality without it also involving us). The attitude "I'm staying out of it!" is fatal, and the upshot is that you too will have to get involved at some point or other. If you want to know what you have to do with a particular situation, ask "(your first name) TOO?" and you will understand why you are involved.

We all want to be happy and successful too. Using this switchword will immerse us in all the events going on around us. Try it and see how you get on, you too will find yourself moving on.

Saying "Me TOO" means you are in agreement with the plans and intentions of another person. In a positive sense you could say, "The same things are going well for me just as they are for you, because I can imagine the ideas you have in your mind for me too." Viewed in a positive sense, you could equally say, "Things will go as well for me as for you because I can imagine myself in your shoes."

AGAIN!/AGAIN?

Say AGAIN three times in a row.

again! again! again!
or
again? again? again?

This switchword demonstrates why certain events repeat themselves and why a particular event is already happening once more. AGAIN reveals where progress is being hampered and why we keep repeating the same experiences, again and again.

If you are unsure whether a particular experience will feature in your future again, you can find out by posing the question "x AGAIN?" You can also say, "I want to treat myself to happiness AGAIN and AGAIN." Remember to exercise caution when choosing the context for this switchword, however. It can be very problematic to tell someone repeatedly about a bad habit. If, for example, you say, "You lied to me again and again!" it should come as no surprise if that action or situation reoccurs, again and again.

Experiencing something over and over again is not meant to be an aspiration in the highest sense. Life is a great adventure that keeps bringing new experiences, again and again.

ADAPT

Say ADAPT eight times in a row.
Take a breathing pause where indicated (**).

adapt   adapt   adapt   adapt   **
adapt   adapt   adapt   adapt

Have you overdone certain things or allowed a situation to get out of hand? Are events spiraling out of control? Can you no longer deal with it all? Is your life no longer on an even keel after working too hard on certain aspects while neglecting others? Would you like to shift down a gear and leave more time for other things? Do you find it difficult to get on with your daily life, and then when you do, find you have nothing left to give for whatever reason? Do you feel as if you have had your eyes closed for a long time and have allowed opportunities to disappear? Just use the switchword ADAPT and your life will miraculously align itself with your rhythm. Say ADAPT to rediscover a connection to current events. It ensures that the resources still at your disposal can be used in the best possible way.

Do you feel that you do not really fit in anywhere? Say ADAPT to be able to fit in in a positive and personal way. "Adapt, but don't give up on yourself" should be your motto. However, it is as well to be careful if, for example, someone tells you to adapt your behavior or risk being fired from the company. People who seem to offend or antagonize everyone around them are focusing on negative things and are losing sight of their own opportunities. Those who fight a constant battle with life should not be surprised when they run at full tilt into the walls they themselves have built. Say ADAPT to put your skills and talents to the best possible use once more.

Discovering your own nature is true revolution!

GIVE

"It is better to give than to receive!" Do you give everything you have only to be surprised when all that effort fails to pay off? The reason lies in how and what you give, since everything will be returned many times over. Give with joy, and allow others to receive that joy. If you give money gladly, you will be rewarded too.

You might think: "I can't give my money to a beggar on the street. I have to work hard for that money. Nobody gives me anything for nothing." Allow people to live their life in the way they choose and give if you can find it in your heart to do so. Have you never wished that somebody would give you some money? Those who are unable to give cannot truly receive. GIVE is the magic word that makes you see what you already have. Being aware of what you have honors and increases its value. Those who give know that they are rich, and will become richer still

Many people are taught about the need for frugality. However, saving for a future rainy day brings forward a potential future shortfall. Imagine how good it would be to be able to pay every bill that lands on the mat immediately. For once, be glad to pay your taxes while recognizing everything that they pay for. It's not a question of how much money you have at this precise moment, but rather about the pleasure with which you recognize what you have. Is it not wonderful to be able to give, just like that, without having to spend too much time thinking about it? Giving makes you happy and contributes to the circulation of wealth. Would you like to help someone but are unsure how? Say GIVE to discover what you can give to the other person to help them resolve their particular situation.

Say the following, for example:

GIVE to patient x
GIVE to pupil x
GIVE to x

Give of your best and you will receive the best in return. Say to yourself, "I always give the best I can, and I am always rewarded with the best." This attitude will stand you in good stead. Give praise, knowledge, and happiness. Give to others all the things that have made your own life worthwhile. Share this philosophy with others. Give without expecting to receive. Those who give will never go without.

SMILE

Say SMILE eight times in a row.
Take a breathing pause where indicated (**).

smile	smile	**
smile	smile	**
smile	smile	**
smile	smile	

Your inner smile banishes anger, hatred, and a desire for revenge. It reveals your awareness of love.

Do you have more enemies than friends? Do you feel hatred, rage, resentment, envy, and similar destructive emotions every day?

From now on, begin your day with the switchword SMILE, and see how the world smiles with you. Smiling triggers an inner certainty that all will be well and that everything has been planned to turn out for the best.

Your inner smile reveals the relaxed attitude of your great being. After all, a smile is infectious. "Smile and the whole world smiles with you." The word SMILE makes you feel happy and reinforces our true certainty about life. Smiling is relaxation in the highest sense!

One of the best things in life is seeing the innocent smile on the face of a happy child. SMILE brings recognition of the truly great and important being within every living thing.

Smile your way to a greater being. If you find yourself in the grip of destructive anger with someone, free yourself with SMILE. Every time a negative feeling threatens to turn you into a lesser being, SMILE and make light in you shine again. Smiling enlightens, in every sense.

FIX

Say FIX four times in a row.

fix   fix   fix   fix

"Dad will fix it." No! You are capable of fixing things that have taken a wrong turn yourself. Simply say the word FIX, and any twist or kink in the truth will be ironed out and fixed. Fix the things that help you to achieve your goals.

Do not try to fix things in a judgmental way but fix upon fixing what is essential, for example:

> FIX person x
> FIX company x
> FIX togetherness

FIX keeps you on target and prevents you from straying from your path. It highlights when there is too great a focus on trivialities. "Judge not, lest ye be judged yourselves" warns that we should not focus too much on the goals of others and how they set out to achieve them, but instead keep our eyes fixed on our own goals. What is right and what is wrong is relative once we have identified our goals. If you have lost your direction, now is the time to reorient yourself once more.

DONE

Say DONE ten times in a row.
Take a breathing pause where indicated (**).

done   done   done   done   done   ******
done   done   done   done   done

"The word, the deed." In reality, things are really only said to be done once we have considered and accepted every aspect of a situation.

DONE enables us to acknowledge any forgotten elements that are required to bring something to a happy conclusion. We can then focus on new projects again.

DONE reveals what we must still do for our personal growth and development, but it also helps us to relax and allow what needs to happen to take place. The word DONE means there will be no need later to berate ourselves for failing to do a particular task.

DONE sharpens our perception of the small and easily overlooked but very important details. Something very trivial may be preventing us from feeling happy, and it often only takes just one small thing to complete our happiness. "I did everything I could, but I'm back at square one!" If this is how you feel, use the switchword DONE.

Say, for example:

  x work DONE
  x project DONE
  x deal DONE

Be ready to give and to do everything, and you will experience your miracle. Once everything has been done, and only then, will our soul decide to move on. We are put here to be everything and to experience true fulfillment. Enlightenment occurs only when everything has been done to serve the greater understanding. Reaching the point where everything has been done is wonderful.

FOR

Say FOR three times in a row.

for   for   for

Are you for or against? FOR is the magic word that helps to redistribute energy and recalibrate a particular imbalance of power. Try using FOR and you will soon be saying, "I'm all for this cause" or "I'm for that solution and for peace." FOR enables you to make a positive personal contribution to a project's success. Being for something does not mean that you are also simultaneously against something else, since being for one thing does not entail being against another. Being against something only reinforces negative forces. Negativity thrives on rejection and repudiation, which can be easily be foisted on you, so be careful if this this happens. Be clear about what you are for, and you will inject energy into what is going on around you.

"I am all for life!" "I am all for love!" "I am all for consciously acknowledging the highest power!"

Simply use the code word FOR from now on, and make sure that you are not against. FOR helps us to move forward and make progress in life, whereas against holds us back once more.

SLOWLY

Say SLOWLY four times in a row.

slowly   slowly   slowly   slowly

Slowly, but surely. Is everything moving too quickly for you? Are you unable to keep up? Are you finding it difficult to keep up to speed with what is happening? Apply the brakes with the switchword SLOWLY. It eases the pressure that holds you back from expressing your true nature. "I just want to make a quick call." "Quick, get your shoes on." "I'll drop by for a quick visit." Think about how often you use the word "quick." Quick highlights that you always feel pressurized and are constantly imposing new forms of pressure on yourself. Once pressure is part of the equation, it hampers flow and blocks progress. Are you finding it increasingly hard to keep up with events? Do you hear yourself saying, "I must just do this or that." You are building the very walls that you will have to climb at a later date.

If you fear you may fail to achieve your goal and are under immense pressure, say the word SLOWLY. With it you can be sure of reaching your goal, one step at a time, leaving you with enough energy to celebrate the victory. SLOWLY makes sure you do not waste energy unnecessarily and reach the point of burn out.

For example, I once had a work colleague who did everything slowly but still completed all her tasks on time. The rest of us were always in a hurry and would run to catch the train while she would stroll to the station in a leisurely manner and still make the train. She would say, "Slowly does it. I will achieve what I want to achieve." And she did just that.

Haste is only ever about fear of missing out. Slow and steady is the way to win the race.

COUNT

Say COUNT five times in a row.

count   count   count   count   count

COUNT is the magic word that multiplies your assets and makes things "count more." COUNT brings appreciation and expansion of your own portfolio of assets. The next time you are checking your bank account and wishing the balance was larger, you know what to do. Would you like to have a larger client base? Would you like to have more friendly people around you? Count and appreciate your gifts now and in reality you will never stop counting them.

"I'm counting on you" is synonymous with "I am alert to you and to your qualities." Can people count on you as well? COUNT activates the wealth that you already have to hand.

DIVINE

"I am simply divine, you are simply divine, we are simply divine!" "You, yourself, are the real miracle." DIVINE is the magic word that nurtures hidden talents and awakens your strength. DIVINE makes miracles possible, the kind that you never even thought existed.

Each of us is so much more than the character that we currently represent or play. DIVINE reveals a new perspective on the true greatness that is reflected in every living creature. Seeing something in a divine light is a wonderful experience. DIVINE reveals how much more we are than a mere function or role. The part that each person plays, or believes they are playing, often detracts from their actual greatness. Have you ever wondered whether you define yourself too much by a particular role, and if people only pay attention to you when you act in the way they think you should? Use DIVINE to free yourself from the role in which you have become entrenched and to find a new purpose. "You are the real miracle."

Activate your divine being, now and forever!

CAUTION

Say CAUTION seven times in a row.

caution   caution   caution   caution
caution   caution   caution

Do you need to pay close attention to something? Are important decisions being made? Is the present moment really important for future plans? CAUTION is the magic word that activates your attention and sharpens all your senses. It mobilizes your 360-degree vision and ensures you are as alert as you need to be to a particular situation. Vigilant and perceptive, you will be in the perfect position to fully grasp the significance of a situation. Nothing will escape you and you will notice things that you might otherwise have missed. Say CAUTION for awareness of small details that can make a big difference.

If you find yourself in a critical situation, for example, something in which your involvement is crucial, you can provide great positive support with the switchword CAUTION.

CAUTION helps you to assess the values of others, and the realization of who you are dealing with may surpise you. CAUTION is the magic word that sparks vigilance and delivers to every living creature conscious presence in the moment, in the here and now.

ACT

Say ACT three times in a row.

act   act   act

Does it feel as though your hands are tied? Have you handed over the reins, leaving your fate in the hands of others? Have you passed responsibility for your well-being in life to someone else? Are you paralyzed by the dependence you once welcomed because you do not know what someone else intends to do? Are you leaving it to those around you to make the decision about what you can and should do?

Do you always hesitate for too long and miss the moment to act that would help you to become fulfilled in life?

ACT activates your inner preparedness and readiness to take action. It enables you to summon all your courage and step up to the plate, secure in the knowledge that what you have to offer will carry the day. Seeing yourself taking action will bring you great joy, because you will have finally overcome the paralyzing passivity that was plaguing you.

HEAL

Say HEAL ten times in a row.
Take a breathing pause where indicated (**).

heal heal heal heal heal **
heal heal heal heal heal

Are you tormented by hurtful things in the past? Are old injuries slow to heal? Are you unable to forget certain events and be happy as a result? The switchword HEAL activates your readiness to be healed at last. Say to yourself, "I am now healed of 'this' for the rest of my life." It is your ability to heal yourself and the conscious recognition of your own strengths that have brought this about. You have won! This healing experience will also boost your future resilience. You have succeeded in making yourself immune and can never be hurt again in the way you were in the past. HEAL makes you happy and grateful.

The magic word HEAL puts you in a position to recognize and resolve an experience from a higher level of consciousness.

REMEMBER

Say REMEMBER nine times in a row.
Take a breathing pause where indicated (******).

remember   remember   remember   ******
remember   remember   remember   ******
remember   remember   remember

"I remember! We remember!" Are you unable to remember the last time you were happy and content? Have you forgotten your happy memories and now live in fear of what the future holds?

Make sure you say to yourself:

REMEMBER happiness, REMEMBER profit,
REMEMBER love, REMEMBER ability

It is an indescribable experience when a memory comes back to us. Of course, we can choose which things to remember, hence the advice to do so with caution, with "foresight." So which memories should be awakened and activated? The conscious choice you make will have a major influence on how you perceive your everyday life. Remember all the good times and great experiences that you have already had. Why should you not achieve in future exactly what you have already managed in the past?

REMEMBER brings memories back in the truest sense. We will remember our true origins. Let's remember our divinity. Let's remember where we came from. It is wonderful when our memories return.

REMEMBER enables you to store away the happiness you are feeling at the very moment that you say it. Say REMEMBER at happy times. Internalize these moments of happiness, and use them to carry you forward on a wave of positivity.

RETREAT

Say RETREAT once.

retreat

When you sense that you may have lost sight of yourself and are giving in too often to anger, say RETREAT with mindful intention. Do you sometimes feel unable to curb your anger? Do you tend to lose control of yourself in certain circumstances, unaware of exactly what you are doing? Do you forget/overlook that things do not have to be this way? RETREAT allows you to exercise self-control and center yourself once more. RETREAT helps with managing ill-disciplined behavior and regaining control. Having taken things too far, do you now want to turn a negative situation to your advantage? RETREAT allows you to take a step back and achieve the conscious perspective you need to do so.

PLAN

Say PLAN nine times in a row.
Take a breathing pause where indicated (**).

plan   plan   plan   plan   plan   **
plan   plan   plan   plan

If positive circumstances appear to be impossible right now, the switch-word PLAN will help to remedy that. Plan your happiness and trust that it will come about in reality.

If certain insights required to turn your dream into reality remain elusive, PLAN will guide those who can help you toward you. We are all bound up with one another in some way and benefit from an exchange of useful knowledge and ideas. The switchword PLAN will ensure that the people whose knowledge will complete your happiness will be drawn toward you. Think of it in terms of building a house. You do not need to be an architect yourself, but you can hire someone with experience and expertise, and in return give them something of value that you have worked for using your own skills. Your house will be completed. PLAN brings the right specialists and experts to your side.

CHOOSE

Say CHOOSE ten times in a row.
Take a breathing pause where indicated (**).

choose   choose   choose   choose   choose   **
choose   choose   choose   choose   choose

Would you like to be able to choose and have choices once more? Or are you overwhelmed with the choices that are available and what life has to offer? Use the switchword CHOOSE to make the correct choice for the present. Allow it to guide you and trust your instinct. If we have choice we can be "spoilt for choice," particularly when we have no real aim in mind, fear making the wrong choice, or are constantly worrying about missing out on the right thing.

If you regret making a particular choice in the past, you will remain stuck in a rut and be likely to lose out. Always stand by your choices but also be aware that you always have a choice. Instead of deciding, choose! CHOOSE activates your real freedom to choose. You can always make a choice, so exercise that right. Every decision involves separation, and separation, in turn, activates desire, preventing us from achieving peace. Every decision is also an act of evaluation. Whenever you make a decision, you will be plagued by doubts about whether you made the right choice, took the right decision, or if you should have gone with an alternative option. Once made, a decision leads to a lack, because doubt prevents fulfillment. However, the code word CHOOSE activates your access to the ideal outcome.

BRING

Say BRING three times in a row.

bring   bring   bring

BRING activates an awareness of what is worthwhile. What will happen if I make this decision or adopt that attitude? What will remaining in this partnership bring? Everything that you do, do not do, or pass on will bring something appropriate back to you. BRING is a messenger from heaven. Since there is no judgement in the universal, cosmic sense, life constantly returns to you what you have given in the past or continue to be ready to give in the present. Choose what you would like to pass on with care, however. To know in advance what something will bring you, say "BRING project" and you will learn what will be given back to you in return.

Life makes no distinctions; it does not distinguish between good and evil, between positive and negative. Our thoughts lead in every conceivable direction and bring the corresponding results. BRING identifies the return. You now have the chance to change your attitude appropriately in order to avoid any future unpleasant surprises. BRING enables you to work out and plan your future. A negative attitude ultimately delivers precious little. BRING also gives you the courage to make decisions and take action. Use BRING and people will realize the contribution you are making and will appreciate you for it.

WITH

Say WITH four times in a row.

with   with   with   with

Would you like to get together with a particular person or thing? Are you keen to work with a certain master, a particular individual? WITH clarifies whether that person is in agreement with your plans, in other words, whether they are in sync with you. Dare to do more. Once you are ready for something and have taken the first step, others will surely want to accompany you on your journey.

Do you sometimes feel that you cannot live with or indeed without something? Are you feeling a little desperate, with no real idea how you are supposed to achieve something? WITH is the magic word that helps you to combine in a positive way the little that you appear to have right now, and manages to create something wonderful with it. You will soon say, "I actually have no idea how I managed to do all this!"

If you are ready to put to good use what may seem to be very little, the outcome will be amazing. Anything can be achieved with what you have. You have everything you need to build a better life. You may only have just become aware of this, but from now on you will begin to be at one with yourself.

Use WITH (first name) to begin each day. For example, say, "I am always on the very best terms with x and I attract into my life people who want to work hard with me for the best reasons."

UP

Say UP twice in a row.

up   up

The magic word UP will lift you up and get rid of any inferiority complexes. If you feel this would be helpful, say your first name and then say UP UP. You will gradually begin to find things less and less of a struggle. Slowly, day by day, you will find you are up to the mark, in the strictest sense of the word. UP provides the motivation to carry on with your journey, to follow your own path, with renewed strength and determination. If you have been spending too much time sitting around as a mere spectator in life, UP will prompt you to carry on with the life plans upon which you have already embarked. The wait is over and things are finally moving! UP activates your genuine efforts and desires.

PROTECT

Say PROTECT three times in a row.

protect   protect   protect

"Protect yourself! You need protection in a situation like that!"

Being overprotected or too guarded can lead you to live life according to the views of others, such as parents or teachers. PROTECT activates your own mind. PROTECT allows you to look after yourself, to be your own protector. Have people given you any warnings about certain situations and told you to take care? The switchword PROTECT activates our inner coping mechanism that helps us to react the best way in unusual situations. We have so many more skills than we are aware of in this world. PROTECT shines a light on old knowledge that can be put to good use now, in the present. Be aware that there is an emergency plan for every contingency but also that failing to believe in this plan will render it useless. Place your trust in this switchword. It activates past knowledge and ancient wisdom, giving the insight that has been hidden away the power to influence events again. We will be able to access abilities and skills that we mastered successfully in past lives.

CONSIDER

Say CONSIDER nine times in a row.
Take a breathing pause where indicated (**).

consider	consider	consider	**
consider	consider	consider	**
consider	consider	consider	

Consider, understand, and archive, or file away. This is the way to collect and store knowledge that will be important at a later date. Would you like to expand your knowledge and develop certain ideas? Use the switchword CONSIDER to gain fresh insight into how to grow and develop on a personal level.

How often do we say, "I must consider what to do next," or "I will have to consider that." Use CONSIDER, and just let go. You already have so much knowledge at your disposal, and now you will be ready to develop it and prepare for higher and more demanding tasks. Knowledge is power and it awakens the interest of your fellow human beings in you.

For example, a thought occurs to you and you consider whether it is a useful addition to your existing knowledge base. If so, more "light-bulb moments" will come and your understanding will grow. Perhaps you recently read a book and have discovered some new ideas. Use CONSIDER to take in information that brings progress. Many things are worth considering. Using CONSIDER separates the important from the trivial. You will recognize whether the information from "outside" is useful in the highest sense and why it will help you to make progress with your personal growth.

CONSIDER x seminar
CONSIDER x performance

BELIEVE

Say BELIEVE six times in a row.
Take a breathing pause where indicated (**).

| believe | ** | believe | ** | believe | ** |
| believe | ** | believe | ** | believe | ** |

You believe that something is possible but are not sure you can manage to achieve it. Many people share this feeling. You have belief but cannot find the faith in yourself to move a mountain of doubt and find fulfillment. Do you lack belief but want to know and understand more? Use the code word BELIEVE to strengthen trust in your own powers. Always remember that faith can move mountains! Say BELIEVE to free yourself from the shackles of pure reason and to see yourself as a greater being. If you cannot believe in yourself, why should others?

Say:

> BELIEVE in love and partnership
> BELIEVE in x
> BELIEVE my child will achieve x

Regain your own belief and you will see the world in a different light.

WORK

Say WORK five times, three times, and then once more.
Take a breathing pause where indicated (**).

work   work   work   work   work   **

work   work   work   **

work

Does nothing seem to work for you? Are you under the impression that everything you say and do is of no real consequence? Do your results never match up with what you intended? Does absolutely nothing work out? The reason for this lies in a negation of your own influence in the past. The negative powers of some people are so strong that nothing affects them. In such cases, use the code word WORK to banish your fears and uncertainty about the invalidity or the "unworkability" of something of your own making. WORK is synonymous with "I shall allow myself to find a solution and achieve victory." WORK breaks through subconscious blockages. It is the ultimate truth that truly works.

"Does what I'm doing work for you?" This question demonstrates a clear sense of a person's insecurity. Many people are controlled by an ego that constantly needs and seeks affirmation from others, which is where a great deal of anger about this self-imposed dependence has its roots. Fears about what works for other people are based on self-doubt, which interferes with the way things pan out. Use the switchword WORK if a past experience of rejection is still hanging over you. Past experiences continue to affect you because you still remember the intimidation that you felt at the time, which has sapped your courage to try again. You do not trust things to work even when it is clear that they will. In instances where you cannot get certain plans out of your head and have not yet quite thought them through, test their potential to succeed with the switchword WORK.

It will activate your courage and belief in your own abilities. "You seem very confident and sure of yourself" is the kind of thing people will say once your attitude has changed. Now you can do anything! Work and enjoy what works for others. Recognize your own validity, your personal workable reality.

SHOW

Say SHOW twelve times in a row.
Take a breathing pause where indicated (******).

show	show	show	show	**
show	show	show	show	**
show	show	show	show	

Are your true qualities never allowed to shine? Do others stop you from demonstrating your skills? Are you never given a chance to get involved and help out? Do you never get the opportunity to introduce yourself? Are you unemployed and yet feel you have so many skills to contribute? The reason behind such an attitude lies in past refusals to show others everything you know. You are now suffering the consequences and are in this world to undergo this unfortunate experience and to heal this attitude. SHOW is the magic word that gets you involved once more and ensures a renewed interest in your qualities from those around you.

"I will show them." SHOW highlights your willingness to be involved in the community and for the common good, and to contribute in the best way that you can. SHOW promotes the communal effort that benefits everyone. SHOW also helps you to help others find answers by showing them your own solutions.

Showing in its widest sense is synonymous with passing things on and consciously recognizing the highest power in every person. Using SHOW demonstrates your great respect for the abilities of others.

Show yourself! Show "yourself" to the world! SHOW helps you to step out of the shadows and into the light.

BOOST

Say BOOST six times in a row.

boost   boost   boost   boost   boost   boost

Do you feel you have to keep your head down and protect yourself? People who always feel the need to shield themselves give others the power to harm them. Fear of being harmed drains and weakens our inner strength. Therefore, instead of seeking to protect yourself, look to empower yourself so that you can act and make conscious choices. Have you succumbed totally to weakness? Do you need to recharge your batteries after wasting energy unnecessarily? Say BOOST to feel reinvigorated and find all the strength you need for life. You will find strength without feeding or fostering weakness. BOOST provides an injection of vitality for those determined to achieve their goals. For example, providing the impetus to eat plenty of nutritious foods (such as those that boost the immune system). You will reap the rewards many times over.

BOOST fortifies us, helping us to put awareness of weakness behind us and to live in strength instead. Rather than feeding on frailty, strength is nourished by acknowledgment of the solution. BOOST activates our inner strength and enables us to make others strong.

When relevant and appropriate, you can say to others:

Be strong and you will win!
Stay strong, you are bound to find a solution!

Use the magic word BOOST when you encounter weakness, for example:

BOOST eye function
BOOST cardiac function

BOOST back muscles
BOOST connective tissue
BOOST trust
BOOST perseverance
BOOST capacity for love

LOVE

Say LOVE eight times in a row.

love   love   love   love
love   love   love   love

"I love the way you are! I love your essence! I love life!" Love is the force that puts an end to all struggle and conflict. "Love your enemies and they will be enemies no more!" But is it possible to love what you reject? With love you can protect yourself from harm. Why do so many people find loving difficult? If your love for yourself (and therefore also your capacity for love) is diminished, it will affect your ability to love. Many people have to force themselves to love. If you cannot love yourself, you will also doubt the love of your partner, child, or friend. You will always be checking whether their actions prove their love. People may seek proof of love in superficial ways, St Valentine's Day being a prime example. If you do not receive a bunch of flowers on this special day, doubt and mistrust may begin to creep in, like a sickness that brings more suffering and uncertainty in its wake. At the same time, love can be felt by simply being with the one you love. Love can be experienced in the first encounter. Look into someone's eyes and feel the moment, and you will know if love is the basis.

Since most people lack the ability for real self-love, they often seek proof of love from others, putting them at constant odds with their partner. "I love myself, I love myself, I love myself just as I am" are the magical words that will make you consciously aware of your own creative powers once more and help you to love yourself. With it, you will take responsibility for everything that you have become. Armed with this attitude, we can banish self-denial and self-doubt, and allow ourselves to change the things around us as we think necessary. Great results can be achieved by saying, "I am the creating and loving power and the awareness and presence of mind that shape, animate, and maintain the health of my body so that its form and function, and my existence in this physical form, are a constant joy for me."

"Love thy neighbor as thyself!" From childhood we are told that others come first and that it is selfish to think of ourselves. It is surprising just how much judgment is tied up with this concept. No one wants to be self-ish, and yet most people are guided only by their ego, which demands their full attention and blinds them to love. We are our own neighbors and responsible to ourselves in the first instance. True love of one's neighbor comes only through self-love. Otherwise, you will be forever testing and checking whether you still have your partner's love. Even if you feel very sure of this love, doubts often arise. "How can this person love me when I find it so difficult to love myself?" This attitude highlights the absurdity that makes life so difficult for many people. When you lack faith in love, heal yourself with love! Love even the unpleasant things in life, and their troubling effects will be mitigated.

Say:

> LOVE x (person)
> LOVE my life
> LOVE work
> LOVE money
> LOVE weather
> LOVE my body
> LOVE x (situation)

"I LOVE all the cells in my body, even those that are cancerous!" Leave nothing out, but instead love even the things that threaten you, since this is true mastery of love.

Love is the strongest healing power,
As love is always the answer.

LIVE/LIFE

Say LIVE seven times in a row or LIFE nine times in a row.
Take a breathing pause where indicated (**).

live   live   live   live   live   live   live   **

or

life   life   life   life   life   life   life   life   life

"I love life! I want to live!" No sooner has life begun than the fear of death creeps in. Countless people miss out on enjoying life by being too preoccupied by its finite nature. Sometimes we may even wonder if we should bother starting something new at all. "Is it really worth it? I might get something out of it, but then again I might not." Many have already given up and in so doing deprive themselves of the opportunity to experience things.

The magic word LIVE revives the spirits in the truest sense of the word. When someone has a fatal illness, for example, their relatives are often the first to give up hope. They start to prepare themselves for what they believe is the inevitable, unable to believe that life goes on. Saying LIVE will help you to regain strength in the present. When we focus on the end, our fatalistic attitude becomes self-fulfilling and our strength and spirit desert us. When someone is sick, unfortunately the rest of the family often turn their relative's condition into a drama instead of helping them by offering strength and belief. Belief in life is also self-fulfilling, boosting vitality. Live! Love! When feeling down, lackluster, and weary, reinvigorate yourself with the magic word LIVE! Even if you are battling a disease, you may derive some relief by saying, "I am the creative present and the conscious mind within me that fills my body with life and now activates every spirit of vitality so that my existence within this body is worth living again!" Life certainly always goes on, in whatever form!

LAUGH

Say LAUGH seven times in a row.

laugh   laugh   laugh   laugh   laugh
laugh   laugh

Do you often feel like crying rather than laughing? Are you sad most days? Does nothing make you really happy? Do you feel down in the dumps just now? When you feel like this, remind yourself that "You just have to laugh." LAUGH helps to banish sad feelings and a sense of loss.

People lose the ability to laugh and are deprived of happiness by past experiences. LAUGH brings freedom from psychological pressure and the compulsion to punish oneself. When going through sad times in the past, you may have suddenly experienced an almost irresistible desire to laugh. LAUGH liberates and resolves negative energy that serves no real purpose and changes nothing. Meet and embrace life with the switchword LAUGH and rediscover your inner confidence. Live, love, and laugh, for your own sake.

WANT

I want!

I WANT activates personal powers of self-determination, but is only effective when used for personal development; for example, "I WANT long-term health and well-being." It will have little effect, however, in instances such as, "I WANT my husband to finally realize that x is the case."

I WANT takes you wherever you want to go, since your personal desires are your future. You now have what you once wanted. Therefore think carefully and with foresight in terms of your desires.

Would you like to put feelings of lethargy behind you and to finally live your life? WANT activates strengths and abilities that have been lying dormant. It promotes a desire for action. A motivation to want more can be stimulated by an idol or hero/heroine, for example, someone you admire. If you would like to be like them and to be capable of doing the kind of amazing things they do, say the name of the person in question and then WANT. You might not think it will work, but just try. You only have to want it! The moment that you choose to want something, things will be set in motion that help you to achieve it.

WANT brings about conscious action to make changes in your life. For example, you are in a difficult situation and decide to seek the help of an expert and make an appointment. A good counsellor is likely to be booked up in advance, so you will have to wait some time before the session can take place. From the moment the appointment is made, however, the solution will start to take shape in your mind. You may well have cracked it and found the solution yourself by the time the appointment comes around and so only need the expert's stamp of approval. You will have firsthand experience of your own abilities if this is what you want.

ABILITY

Say ABILITY six times in a row.

ability   ability   ability   ability   ability   ability

ABILITY is about having the capability to do certain things. Believe in your ABILITY and you can do anything. Have people long told you that you are good for nothing? If so, it is a great shame if you also share their opinion. Use the code word ABILITY to trigger your capabilities and see how you become more courageous and dare to venture into new ways of expressing your creativity. ABILITY activates courage and self-belief.

Say, "I dare to believe in more (or all) of my abilities once more."

Armed with this attitude, you can become an expert in something. There is no need to compare your ability with that of others, since you have long been able to do what they can. Trust in the greatest ability and become a connoisseur or expert.

MASTER

Say MASTER eleven times in a row.
Take a breathing pause where indicated (**).

master	master	master	master	**
master	master	master	master	**
master	master	master		

No master has yet fallen from a clear blue sky, but every master wants their skill levels to reach sky-high. Masters choose their goal, but the way they achieve it remains a mystery. Are you genuinely ready to be a master? If so, your apprenticeship will begin now. Would you like to be acclaimed and admired for your achievements? MASTER is the code word that will make of you more than you could ever dare to imagine. MASTER helps you to overcome conventionality. A master does not live as the ordinary people do, the masses, but nor does a master interfere in the course of people's lives, respecting the meaning and self-determination of every living being. MASTER activates a broad spectrum of abilities. Should you wish to be a master in a particular field or sphere, ask for support: "I would like to master this project and ask the Master (Jesus or a particular saint, for example) to use their experience to assist my efforts." More is required of you than a desire for the ordinary, the conventional things.

The switchword MASTER prepares you for true mastery. Masters pass on their knowledge, but they do not do so by teaching. Instead, they reinforce the belief of others in their own mastery and strengthen them in all their masterful being. A master expects everything from you because they know you are capable of anything. Your soul has already come a long way, and you have now been placed on this Earth to do justice to your own true greatness. MASTER reveals how to achieve this.

PRAISE

Say PRAISE once

praise

"Praised be the beauty of this day! Praised be your work! Praised be the solution to this issue!"

Praising something in our lives, appreciating its quality and worth, will bring us a sense of joy and calm.

PRAISE enables us to grow in the quality of victory without many more demands being made of us.

To be awarded praise is to be blessed with a distinction. PRAISE therefore activates great victory and fosters the desire for great achievement. PRAISE enables such qualities to grow without limit and to develop in new dimensions.

Instead of "Praise the Lord," we could say any of the following: "Praised be your/my being." "Praise the divine power within you." "Praised be the miraculous omnipotence of your spirit." These are statements that encourage an awareness of those qualities that are present and in so doing help to strengthen our reality.

Praised be the highest power within me
Praised be my existence
Praised be my whole being

"Praised be the miracle of life revealed in each and every moment."

Be the best you possibly can be, make the very best of yourself, and express it in actions. Praise the miracle of love. Praise the choice of your life. Praise the work of your fellow human beings, and you will earn great respect. You will pay a high price only if you neglect yourself, so make sure you praise your own existence too.

ALLOW

Say ALLOW five times in a row.

allow   allow   allow   allow   allow

ALLOW raises awareness of a future harvest and increases its potential.

To ensure your actions have value and are meaningful and fruitful, use the switchword ALLOW. Your plans will bring visible benefits. ALLOW enables you to identify what will bring a gain of some kind and what will not. Be generous and grant yourself and those around you only the best. If you find yourself being tormented by envy and jealousy, suppress this negative and disruptive attitude by saying ALLOW and become a benefactor to others once again. Bring out your altruistic nature once more. ALLOW also creates promising opportunities, so make the best use of this immediate potential. Seize the day! If an opportunity presents itself to you today, life is demonstrating the need to strike while the iron is hot, to take advantage of the chance for freedom and resolution. ALLOW activates gain and growth. People who procrastinate are simply punishing themselves, depriving themselves of opportunity. ALLOW yourself happiness. ALLOW yourself freedom to choose. ALLOW yourself pleasure.

STEER

Say STEER eight times in a row.
Take a breathing pause where indicated (**).

steer   steer   steer   steer   **
steer   steer   steer   steer

Is your life controlled by others? Must you always play second fiddle? Do you have to keep changing your plans because your boss, for example, wants to move in another direction? Do you wish you could finally go your own way? Can you hand over the reins to someone else without feeling controlled by them? You may be able to STEER things in the right direction more wisely and effectively than you can possibly imagine. The switchword STEER will free you from the compulsion to follow someone else's path. Use STEER and take the lead. You will be in the company of those following the same path as you.

STEER requires trust. A good exercise to test the extent of the trust between you and your partner, for example, involves wearing a blindfold and falling back into their arms so they can catch you. You can also carry out this exercise with your child. It would be a matter of some concern should your child be unable to trust you, but finding this out would reveal where work is needed.

Are you constantly afraid of going in the wrong direction with your partner, yet are always talked into agreeing to things? Use STEER to clarify the extent to which your intentions and life plan chime with theirs. "You row, God steers!" There is more to this saying than you might think. If the path ahead appears blocked in a particular direction and progress seems to have come to a standstill, say STEER to be guided to the place where you can find resolution and fulfillment. STEER helps when you have lost your bearings and are unsure which direction to take on life's path. STEER activates your inner compass, ensuring you reach your goal safely and quickly. If you have strayed from your path, STEER can guide you back. Are you easily distracted by people, events, and things that still lead you nowhere? Do you find it difficult to keep your thoughts focused because your mind is occupied by people and things that have challenged your ego? Control this tendency right away and regain your presence of mind by saying, "My mind is free of pointless thoughts."

STOP

Say STOP three times in a row.

stop   stop   stop

Do you feel compelled to do certain things? Are you always doing things that you do not really want to do? Or are there things that you simply cannot leave alone? Habits become compulsions that stand in the way of a new, better way of life. Developing a habit, where an action becomes habitual and repetitive, can be very unwelcome. For example, if you feel compelled to drink alcohol or smoke cigarettes, making you a slave to your compulsion.

Our brains have enormous potential, but when we are slaves to compulsive behavior, the same synapses are being constantly activated. By repeating something over and over again, our "wheels" become stuck in a groove and we follow the same track. The code word STOP will disrupt this repetitive cycle. It will help you to master your compulsions more quickly and easily. Whenever you feel tempted to give in to compulsive behavior say STOP three times.

HIDE

Say HIDE three times in a row.

hide   hide   hide

Do you often find yourself unable to hide unwanted feelings and impluses in the presence of certain people? Does this interfere with and stop you from being able to do something or completing a current task? HIDE regulates the physical signs in the body that might reveal fear or excitement.

HIDE insecurity
HIDE inexperience
HIDE past x
HIDE x situation

Hide the things that are not intended for the eyes of others. Use HIDE to help heal old wounds by removing reminders of them to make sure your attention is not being constantly drawn back to them.

LOOK

Say LOOK seven times, five times, then three times in a row.
Take a breathing pause where indicated (**).

look   look   look   look   look   look   look   **
look   look   look   look   look   **
look   look   look

To look is much more than to see; it is to see with the heart and triggers our clairvoyant powers. When we observe a situation and assess it, we only see the things we think belong in that context. Thinking blurs our ability to view the bigger picture. We think what we see. Thinking is "image-ination" and will cause us to fixate on a single mental image, on just a part of a whole event. The switchword LOOK activates seeing without thinking.

Have you lost track of what is going on? Can you no longer view a situation objectively? Can you only see one side of things and do you tend to ignore the other? LOOK enables you to "see" with your intuition and feelings again and to realize that you can observe something without passing judgment. You will regain your awareness and find an overview of the essential big picture.

COST

Say COST twice in a row.

cost   cost

"I am ready for anything, whatever the cost." This could be your new motto. As long as we think in terms of cost/benefit, we live ordinary lives and deprive ourselves of new experiences. COST is about daring to do something new. "What will it cost me to try?" You will probably have asked yourself this question at some time or other, and perhaps dared to do something and doubtless benefited from it.

Are you anxious about the cost of something and scale back your ambitions as a result? If so, you have lost faith in the wonderful expansion of your world/in the great opportunities that await you. Say COST to bring experiences that will not cost you the Earth. You are bound to cover your costs! Are you scared it might cost you your reputation or your true love? Do you even fear it might cost you your life? COST makes it clear what you can and should now dare to do by revealing your fears, no more and no less. If something is costing you too much effort, you are approaching it with the wrong attitude. You now have the option to use COST to identify profit/benefit or loss. Say COST and listen to what your heart tells you. See how your efforts and bravery are rewarded. If you see only the cost and not the profit or benefit, you are bound to lose out. Examine your own attitude. What others think will only impact upon your life if you let it. It is what you think that really matters. People who focus on reducing costs do not really believe in growth. Those who optimize their own costs balance the ratio of giving and taking only with profit in mind. Those who live at the cost of others have already given up on their own personal growth. Enjoy the opportunities that life presents to you without counting only the cost.

AMEN

Say AMEN once.

Amen

AMEN is the blessing of everything that has gone before (and has been said before). AMEN is the end and also the beginning. If an experience is completed through an insight, new possibilities open up because life goes on, in all its indescribable magnificence. Just as in several traditions of worship amen is said in response or as a conclusion to a prayer, we should finish every day by reviewing and taking stock. Before you fall asleep, give thanks for the day and for the insights you have gained. But if you cannot find the words, simply say AMEN, as this is the best way to bring events to a close. It will help you to start the next day on the right foot.

MORE KEY SWITCHWORDS

OM–I am awakens the creative presence within us and supports the highest power. I am the creative presence that determines my existence in the way that I experience it right now.

ASK awakens the power of conscious effort and desire. Ask and it shall be given, and no asking shall be in vain. All requests should be clearly formulated, however.

THANK awakens awareness of existing qualities. Life is the gratitude of your attitude! Say, "Thank you for the riches that your presence brings to my life."

NOW awakens your awareness of current opportunities and options, and puts an end to waiting. It is "now or never." If you do not start now, you are sure to regret it later at some point.

AHA will get your opponent or opposite number thinking!

PEACE BE WITH YOU brings your struggle with yourself and those around you to an end. PEACE BE WITH YOU mitigates conflict and destruction, and defuses abusive plans.

GRACE brings the potential to start again from the beginning. It asks for another chance so that a failed enterprise may be successful at a second attempt. "I am graced with abilities in the field of x." Feel the grace of and be guided by the highest power within you.

ALWAYS makes things eternal. Be careful when using this switchword, depending on the context in which you use it. The result could be that you find yourself bound to something you did not desire.

HALT puts a stop to things to prevent pointless waste of energy.

ONWARD promotes your personal creativity and delivers new possibilities. If you are unsure of the next step, the code word ONWARD will soon identify what will help you on your way. Things will always move onward, but it is up to you to determine the point at which you have reached your destination.

HEY brings a temporary hiatus so that you can steer matters in the direction you have planned and determined yourself.

PERIOD (FULL STOP) helps to bring something to an end because no further action is required, there is nothing more to add. It brings closure to events to help you digest and process what you have just taken in. When things get too much, take time out. Say PERIOD and then once you are ready to carry on, say ONWARD.

CHANGE resolves current situations and helps to optimize them. When plagued by fear and self-doubt, relieve these feelings by using CHANGE. If doubt is really gnawing away at you, you may have to use this code word many times before finally being able to put aside any last limiting misgivings. Do not let anything stop you or stand in the way of your happiness; remember the obstacle is always yourself.

MOVE counteracts paralysis and inaction, freeing you from the attitudes that block your path. It has a stimulating effect on the brain. It may give you the impetus to move things on in your life or to move your body in different ways.

INDEX OF SWITCHWORDS

ABOUT THE AUTHOR

Franziska Krattinger (1957–2013) was a Swiss author and life coach. From an early age she had the ability to see the auras of both people and animals, and this marked the starting point for her insights into spiritual mysteries. For over twenty years she used her abilities with great success to counsel people and give seminars in life- and consciousness-development.

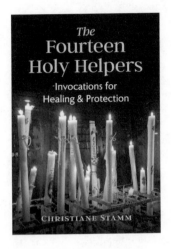

The Fourteen Holy Helpers are a group of Catholic saints who are venerated because their intercession has been shown to be particularly effective in difficult times. The author shares 15 prayers—one for each Holy Helper, and one prayer to call on all 14 Helpers together—to invoke these saints and ask for their spiritual assistance.

In this full-color pocket guide featuring beautiful animal photos, the authors introduce 45 important spirit animals alphabetically and explore their wisdom. They provide a meditative journey to help you discover which animal is your personal soul companion and suggest exercises to intuitively find the right power animal for a given situation.

Christiane Stamm

The Fourteen Holy Helpers

Invocations for Healing and Protection

Paperback, 112 pages

ISBN 978-1-64411-469-8

Phillip Kansa
*https://www.innertraditions.com/
author/phillip-kansa*;
Elke Kirchner-Young
*https://www.innertraditions.com/
author/elke-kirchner-young*

Animal Spirit Wisdom

A Pocket Reference to 45 Power Animals

Paperback, full-color throughout,
112 pages

ISBN 978-1-64411-115-4

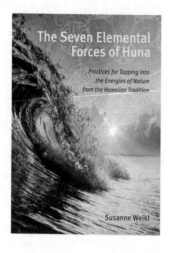 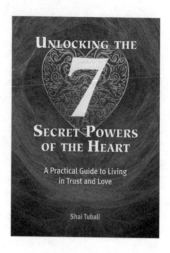

Huna is an ancient shamanic tradition from Hawaii that recognizes seven elemental Nature powers into which we can tap anywhere and at any time. Connect your soul with water, fire, wind, rock, plants, animals, and beings of light. The easy to implement exercises, techniques, and rituals presented in this book will enable you to draw on the strength of the natural forces for empowerment.

Susanne Weikl

The Seven Elemental Forces of Huna
Practices for Tapping into the Energies of Nature from the Hawaiian Tradition

Paperback, full-color throughout, 128 pages

ISBN 978-1-62055-885-0

The heart, often perceived as our most vulnerable and fragile organ, is in fact the source of our greatest potential. This book will unveil the seven secret powers of the heart and help you to discover how to awaken them, leading to a deep sense of peace, balance, and fulfillment and enable you to approach life from a place of trust and love.

Shai Tubali

Unlocking the Seven Secret Powers of the Heart
A Practical Guide to Living in Trust and Love

Paperback, full-color throughout, 128 pages

ISBN 978-1-62055-812-6

Discover everything you need to know about the luminous infinity symbol. Use the many simple exercises contained in this book for decision-making, improving your relationships, reconnecting the analytical and the emotional sides of your brain, and much more. The lemniscate can be used in a wide variety of ways.

Barbara Heider-Rauter

The Power of the Infinity Symbol

Working with the Lemniscate for Ultimate Harmony and Balance

Paperback, full-color throughout, 128 pages

ISBN 978-1-84409-752-4

Powerful yet concise, this revolutionary guide summarizes the Hawaiian ritual of forgiveness and offers methods for immediately creating positive effects in everyday life. Ho'oponopono consists of four consequent magic sentences: "I am sorry. Please forgive me. I love you. Thank you." By addressing issues using these simple sentences we are able to own our feelings, and accept unconditional love, so that unhealthy situations transform into favorable experiences.

Ulrich Emil Duprée

Ho'oponopono

The Hawaiian forgiveness ritual as the key to your life's fulfillment

Paperback, full-color throughout, 96 pages

ISBN 978-1-84409-597-1

For further information and to request a book catalog contact:
Inner Traditions, One Park Street, Rochester, Vermont 05767

Earthdancer Books is an Inner Traditions imprint
Phone: +1-800-246-8648, customerservice@innertraditions.com
www.earthdancerbooks.com • www.innertraditions.com

EARTHDANCER

AN INNER TRADITIONS IMPRINT